Sustainability of Ground-Water Resources

U.S. Geological Survey Circular 1186

by   William M. Alley
     Thomas E. Reilly
     O. Lehn Franke

Denver, Colorado
1999

U.S. DEPARTMENT OF THE INTERIOR
BRUCE BABBITT, Secretary

U.S. GEOLOGICAL SURVEY
Charles G. Groat, Director

U.S. GOVERNMENT PRINTING OFFICE : 1999

Free on application to the
U.S. Geological Survey
Branch of Information Services
Box 25286
Denver, CO 80225-0286

Library of Congress Cataloging-in-Publications Data

Alley, William M.
　　Sustainability of ground-water resources / by William M. Alley, Thomas E. Reilly, and
O. Lehn Franke.
　　　p. cm -- (U.S. Geological Survey circular : 1186)
　　Includes bibliographical references.
　　1. Groundwater--United States. 2. Water resources development--United States. I.
Reilly, Thomas E. II. Franke, O. Lehn. III. Title. IV. Series.

GB1015 .A66 1999
333.91'040973--dc21
　　　　　　　　　　　　　　　　　　　　　　　　　99–040088
　　　　　　　　　　　　　　　　　　　　　ISBN 0–607–93040–3

FOREWORD

*T*oday, many concerns about the Nation's ground-water resources involve questions about their future sustainability. The sustainability of ground-water resources is a function of many factors, including depletion of ground-water storage, reductions in streamflow, potential loss of wetland and riparian ecosystems, land subsidence, saltwater intrusion, and changes in ground-water quality. Each ground-water system and development situation is unique and requires an analysis adjusted to the nature of the existing water issues. The purpose of this Circular is to illustrate the hydrologic, geologic, and ecological concepts that must be considered to assure the wise and sustainable use of our precious ground-water resources. The report is written for a wide audience of persons interested or involved in the protection and sustainable use of the Nation's water resources.

Charles G. Groat, Director
U.S. Geological Survey

CONTENTS

BOXES

Under natural conditions, water levels in wells completed in many confined aquifers rise above the land surface, resulting in artesian flow. The well shown in the photograph was drilled near Franklin, Virginia, in 1941 to a depth of about 600 feet in confined aquifers. The initial water level in the well was about 7 feet above land surface. The above-ground structure shown in the photograph (Cederstrom, 1945) was built in the 1940's as a creative solution to measure the water level in this well. Measurements at the well were discontinued in 1960. Today, measurements at other nearby wells indicate that water levels are now 150 to more than 200 feet below land surface.

Sustainability of Ground-Water Resources

by **William M. Alley**
Thomas E. Reilly
O. Lehn Franke

INTRODUCTION

Ground water is one of the Nation's most important natural resources. It provides about 40 percent of the Nation's public water supply. In addition, more than 40 million people, including most of the rural population, supply their own drinking water from domestic wells. As a result, ground water is an important source of drinking water in every State (Figure 1). Ground water is also the source of much of the water used for irrigation. It is the Nation's principal reserve of freshwater and represents much of the potential future water supply. Ground water is a major contributor to flow in many streams and rivers and has a strong influence on river and wetland habitats for plants and animals.

The pumpage of fresh ground water in the United States in 1995 was estimated to be approximately 77 billion gallons per day (Solley and others, 1998), which is about 8 percent of the estimated 1 trillion gallons per day of natural recharge to the Nation's ground-water systems (Nace, 1960). From an overall national perspective, the ground-water resource appears ample. Locally, however, the availability of ground water varies widely. Moreover, only a part of the ground water stored in the subsurface can be recovered by wells in an economic manner and without adverse consequences.

Ground water is one of the Nation's most important natural resources.

1

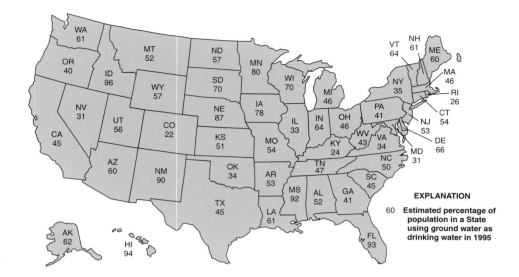

Figure 1. Ground water is an important source of drinking water for every State. (U.S. Geological Survey, 1998.)

EXPLANATION

60 Estimated percentage of population in a State using ground water as drinking water in 1995

The construction of surface reservoirs has slowed considerably in recent years (Figure 2). As surface-water resources become fully developed and appropriated, ground water commonly offers the only available source for new development. In many areas of the United States, however, pumping of ground water has resulted in significant depletion of ground-water storage. Furthermore, ground water and surface water are closely related and in many areas comprise a single resource (Winter and others, 1998). Ground-water pumping can result in reduced river flows, lower lake levels, and reduced discharges to wetlands and springs, causing concerns about drinking-water supplies, riparian areas, and critical aquatic habitats. Increasingly, attention is being placed on how to manage ground water (and surface water) in a sustainable manner (Downing, 1998; Sophocleous, 1998; Gelt and others, 1999).

Resource sustainability has proved to be an elusive concept to define in a precise manner and with universal applicability. In this report, we define ground-water sustainability as development and use of ground water in a manner that can be maintained for an indefinite time without causing unacceptable environmental, economic, or social consequences. The definition of "unacceptable consequences" is largely subjective and may involve a large number of criteria. Furthermore, ground-water sustainability must be defined within the context of the complete hydrologic system of which ground water is a part. For example, what may be established as an acceptable rate of ground-water withdrawal with respect to changes in ground-water levels may reduce the availability of surface water to an unacceptable level. Some key goals related to ground-water sustainability in the United Kingdom are listed in Figure 3. These goals apply equally well in the United States.

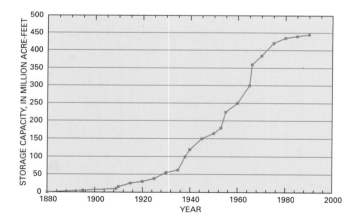

Figure 2. Total surface-water reservoir capacity in the conterminous United States from 1880 to 1990. (Modified from Solley, 1995.)

THE PRIORITIES FOR GROUND-WATER MANAGEMENT

- SUSTAINABLE LONG-TERM YIELDS FROM AQUIFERS
- EFFECTIVE USE OF THE LARGE VOLUME OF WATER STORED IN AQUIFERS
- PRESERVATION OF GROUND-WATER QUALITY
- PRESERVATION OF THE AQUATIC ENVIRONMENT BY PRUDENT ABSTRACTION OF GROUND WATER
- INTEGRATION OF GROUND WATER AND SURFACE WATER INTO A COMPREHENSIVE WATER AND ENVIRONMENTAL MANAGEMENT SYSTEM

TO PROTECT A PRICELESS NATIONAL ASSET

Figure 3. *Vision statement of priorities for ground-water management in the United Kingdom. (Modified from Downing, 1998.)*

Perhaps the most important attribute of the concept of ground-water sustainability is that it fosters a long-term perspective to management of ground-water resources. Several factors reinforce the need for a long-term perspective. First, ground water is not a nonrenewable resource, such as a mineral or petroleum deposit, nor is it completely renewable in the same manner and timeframe as solar energy. Recharge of ground water from precipitation continually replenishes the ground-water resource but may do so at much smaller rates than the rates of ground-water withdrawals. Second, ground-water development may take place over many years; thus, the effects of both current and future development must be considered in any water-management strategy. Third, the effects of ground-water pumping tend to manifest themselves slowly over time. For example, the full effects of pumping on surface-water resources may not be evident for many years after pumping begins. Finally, losses from ground-water storage must be placed in the context of the period over which sustainability needs to be achieved. Ground-water withdrawals and replenishment by recharge usually are variable both seasonally and from year to year. Viewing the ground-water system through time, a long-term approach to sustainability may involve frequent temporary withdrawals from ground-water storage that are balanced by intervening additions to ground-water storage.

Ground water is not a nonrenewable resource, such as a mineral or petroleum deposit, nor is it completely renewable in the same manner and timeframe as solar energy.

Three terms that have long been associated with ground-water sustainability need special mention; namely, safe yield, ground-water mining, and overdraft. The term "safe yield" commonly is used in efforts to quantify sustainable ground-water development. The term should be used with respect to specific effects of pumping, such as water-level declines, reduced streamflow, and degradation of water quality. The consequences of pumping should be assessed for each level of development, and safe yield taken as the maximum pumpage for which the consequences are considered acceptable. The term "ground-water mining" typically refers to a prolonged and progressive decrease in the amount of water stored in a ground-water system, as may occur, for example, in heavily pumped aquifers in arid and semiarid regions. Ground-water mining is a hydrologic term without connotations about water-management practices (U.S. Water Resources Council, 1980). The term "overdraft" refers to withdrawals of ground water from an aquifer at rates considered to be excessive and therefore carries the value judgment of over-development. Thus, overdraft may refer to ground-water mining that is considered excessive as well as to other undesirable effects of ground-water withdrawals.

In some situations, the focus of attention may be on extending the useful life of an aquifer as opposed to achieving long-term sustainability. This situation—for which the term ground-water mining is perhaps most fitting—is not addressed specifically in this report; however, many of the same hydrologic principles that we discuss herein still apply.

This introductory discussion indicates that the concept of ground-water sustainability and its application to real situations is multifaceted and complex. The effects of many human activities on ground-water resources and on the broader environment need to be clearly understood.

We begin by reviewing some pertinent facts and concepts about ground water and some common misconceptions about water budgets and ground-water sustainability. Individual chapters then focus on the interactions between ground water and surface water, on ground-water storage, and on ground-water quality as each aspect relates to the sustainability of ground-water resources. We conclude by discussing the importance of ground-water data, uses of ground-water models, and strategies to meet the challenges posed in assuring sustainable use of ground-water resources.

Throughout the report, we emphasize that development of ground-water resources has consequences to hydrologic and related environmental systems. We discuss relevant concepts and field examples in the body of the text, and provide more technical discussion of special topics and additional field examples in "boxes." An exception is the next special section, "General Facts and Concepts about Ground Water." Many readers familiar with ground-water concepts will want to go directly to the chapter on "Ground-Water Development, Sustainability, and Water Budgets."

"If sustainable development is to mean anything, such development must be based on an appropriate understanding of the environment—an environment where knowledge of water resources is basic to virtually all endeavors."

Report on Water Resources Assessment, WMO/UNESCO, 1991

GENERAL FACTS AND CONCEPTS ABOUT GROUND WATER

The following review of some basic facts and concepts about ground water serves as background for the discussion of ground-water sustainability.

- **Ground water occurs almost everywhere beneath the land surface.** The widespread occurrence of potable ground water is the reason that it is used as a source of water supply by about one-half the population of the United States, including almost all of the population that is served by domestic water-supply systems.

- **Natural sources of freshwater that become ground water are (1) areal recharge from precipitation that percolates through the unsaturated zone to the water table (Figure 4) and (2) losses of water from streams and other bodies of surface water such as lakes and wetlands**. Areal recharge ranges from a tiny fraction to about one-half of average annual precipitation. Because areal recharge occurs over broad areas, even small average rates of recharge (for example, a few inches per year) represent significant volumes of inflow to ground water. Streams and other surface-water bodies may either gain water from ground water or lose (recharge) water to ground water. Streams commonly are a significant source of recharge to ground water downstream from mountain fronts and steep hillslopes in arid and semiarid areas and in karst terrains (areas underlain by limestone and other soluble rocks).

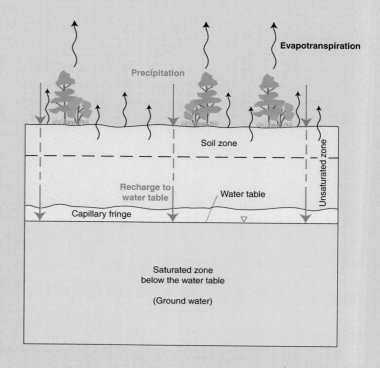

- **The top of the subsurface ground-water body, the water table, is a surface, generally below the land surface, that fluctuates seasonally and from year to year in response to changes in recharge from precipitation and surface-water bodies.** On a regional scale, the configuration of the water table commonly is a subdued replica of the land-surface topography. The depth to the water table varies. In some settings, it can be at or near the land surface; for example, near bodies of surface water in humid climates. In other settings, the depth to the water table can be hundreds of feet below land surface.

Figure 4. *The unsaturated zone, capillary fringe, water table, and saturated zone.*

Water beneath the land surface occurs in two principal zones, the unsaturated zone and the saturated zone. In the unsaturated zone, the spaces between particle grains and the cracks in rocks contain both air and water. Although a considerable amount of water can be present in the unsaturated zone, this water cannot be pumped by wells because capillary forces hold it too tightly.

In contrast to the unsaturated zone, the voids in the saturated zone are completely filled with water. The approximate upper surface of the saturated zone is referred to as the water table. Water in the saturated zone below the water table is referred to as ground water. Below the water table, the water pressure is high enough to allow water to enter a well as the water level in the well is lowered by pumping, thus permitting ground water to be withdrawn for use.

Between the unsaturated zone and the water table is a transition zone, the capillary fringe. In this zone, the voids are saturated or almost saturated with water that is held in place by capillary forces.

- **Ground water commonly is an important source of surface water.** The contribution of ground water to total streamflow varies widely among streams, but hydrologists estimate the average contribution is somewhere between 40 and 50 percent in small and medium-sized streams. Extrapolation of these numbers to large rivers is not straightforward; however, the ground-water contribution to all streamflow in the United States may be as large as 40 percent. Ground water also is a major source of water to lakes and wetlands.

- **Ground water serves as a large subsurface water reservoir.** Of all the freshwater that exists, about 75 percent is estimated to be stored in polar ice and glaciers and about 25 percent is estimated to be stored as ground water. Freshwater stored in rivers, lakes, and as soil moisture amounts to less than 1 percent of the world's freshwater. The reservoir aspect of some large ground-water systems can be a key factor in the development of these systems. A large ratio of total ground-water storage either to ground-water withdrawals by pumping or to natural discharge is one of the potentially useful characteristics of a ground-water system and enables water supplies to be maintained through long periods of drought. On the other hand, high ground-water use in areas of little recharge sometimes causes widespread declines in ground-water levels and a significant decrease in storage in the ground-water reservoir.

- **Velocities of ground-water flow generally are low and are orders of magnitude less than velocities of streamflow.** The movement of ground water normally occurs as slow seepage through the pore spaces between particles of unconsolidated earth materials or through networks of fractures and solution openings in consolidated rocks. A velocity of 1 foot per day or greater is a high rate of movement for ground water, and ground-water velocities can be as low as 1 foot per year or 1 foot per decade. In contrast, velocities of streamflow generally are measured in feet per second. A velocity of 1 foot per second equals about 16 miles per day. The low velocities of ground-water flow can have important implications, particularly in relation to the movement of contaminants.

- **Under natural conditions, ground water moves along flow paths from areas of recharge to areas of discharge at springs or along streams, lakes, and wetlands.** Discharge also occurs as seepage to bays or the ocean in coastal areas, and as transpiration by plants whose roots extend to near the water table. The three-dimensional body of earth material saturated with moving ground water that extends from areas of recharge to areas of discharge is referred to as a ground-water-flow system (Figure 5).

Figure 5. *A local scale ground-water-flow system.*

In this local scale ground-water-flow system, inflow of water from areal recharge occurs at the water table. Outflow of water occurs as (1) discharge to the atmosphere as ground-water evapotranspiration (transpiration by vegetation rooted at or near the water table or direct evaporation from the water table when it is at or close to the land surface) and (2) discharge of ground water directly through the streambed. Short, shallow flow paths originate at the water table near the stream. As distance from the stream increases, flow paths to the stream are longer and deeper. For long-term average conditions, inflow to this natural ground-water system must equal outflow.

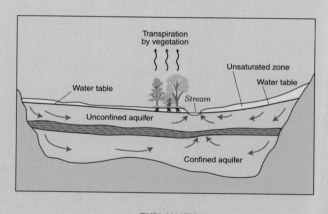

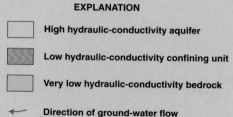

EXPLANATION

High hydraulic-conductivity aquifer

Low hydraulic-conductivity confining unit

Very low hydraulic-conductivity bedrock

← Direction of ground-water flow

- **The areal extent of ground-water-flow systems varies from a few square miles or less to tens of thousands of square miles.** The length of ground-water-flow paths ranges from a few feet to tens, and sometimes hundreds, of miles. A deep ground-water-flow system with long flow paths between areas of recharge and discharge may be overlain by, and in hydraulic connection with, several shallow, more local, flow systems (Figure 6). Thus, the definition of a ground-water-flow system is to some extent subjective and depends in part on the scale of a study.

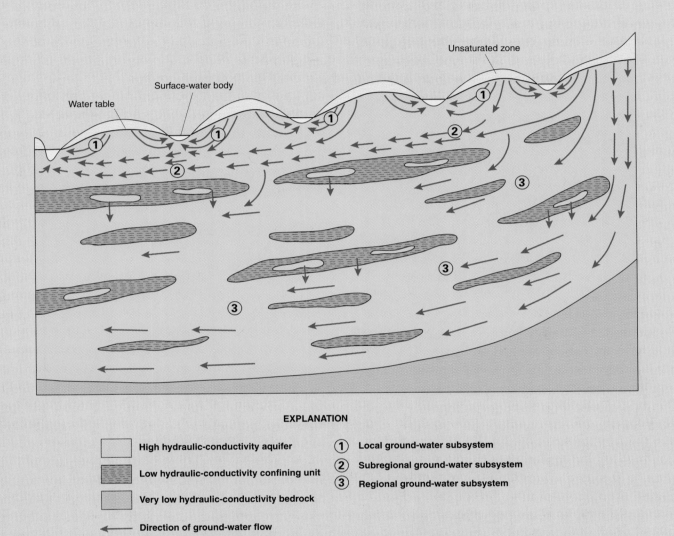

EXPLANATION

High hydraulic-conductivity aquifer

Low hydraulic-conductivity confining unit

Very low hydraulic-conductivity bedrock

Direction of ground-water flow

(1) Local ground-water subsystem

(2) Subregional ground-water subsystem

(3) Regional ground-water subsystem

Figure 6. *A regional ground-water-flow system that comprises subsystems at different scales and a complex hydrogeologic framework. (Modified from Sun, 1986.)*

Significant features of this depiction of part of a regional ground-water-flow system include (1) local ground-water subsystems in the upper water-table aquifer that discharge to the nearest surface-water bodies (lakes or streams) and are separated by ground-water divides beneath topographically high areas; (2) a subregional ground-water subsystem in the water-table aquifer in which flow paths originating at the water table do not discharge into the nearest surface-water body but into a more distant one; and (3) a deep, regional ground-water-flow subsystem that lies beneath the water-table subsystems and is hydraulically connected to them. The hydrogeologic framework of the flow system exhibits a complicated spatial arrangement of high hydraulic-conductivity aquifer units and low hydraulic-conductivity confining units. The horizontal scale of the figure could range from tens to hundreds of miles.

- **The age (time since recharge) of ground water varies in different parts of ground-water-flow systems.** The age of ground water increases steadily along a particular flow path through the ground-water-flow system from an area of recharge to an area of discharge. In shallow, local-scale flow systems, ages of ground water at areas of discharge can vary from less than a day to a few hundred years. In deep, regional flow systems with long flow paths (tens of miles), ages of ground water may reach thousands or tens of thousands of years.

- **Surface and subsurface earth materials are highly variable** in their degree of particle consolidation, the size of particles, the size and shape of pore or open spaces between particles and between cracks in consolidated rocks, and in the mineral and chemical composition of the particles. Ground water occurs both in loosely aggregated and unconsolidated materials, such as sand and gravel, and in consolidated rocks, such as sandstone, limestone, granite, and basalt.

- **Earth materials vary widely in their ability to transmit and store ground water.** The ability of earth materials to transmit ground water (quantified as hydraulic conductivity) varies by orders of magnitude and is determined by the size, shape, interconnectedness, and volume of spaces between solids in the different types of materials. For example, the interconnected pore spaces in sand and gravel are larger than those in finer grained sediments, and the hydraulic conductivity of sand and gravel is larger than the hydraulic conductivity of the finer grained materials. The ability of earth materials to store ground water also varies among different types of materials. For example, the volume of water stored in cracks and fractures per unit volume of granite is much smaller than the volume stored per unit volume in the intergranular spaces between particles of sand and gravel.

- **Wells are the principal direct window to study the subsurface environment.** Not only are wells used to pump ground water for many purposes, they also provide essential information about conditions in the subsurface. For example, wells (1) allow direct measurement of water levels in the well, (2) allow sampling of ground water for chemical analysis, (3) provide access for a large array of physical measurements in the borehole (borehole geophysical logging) that give indirect information on the properties of the fluids and earth materials in the neighborhood of the well, and (4) allow hydraulic testing (aquifer tests) of the earth materials in the neighborhood of the well to determine local values of their transmitting and storage properties. In addition, earth materials can be sampled directly at any depth during the drilling of the well.

- **Pumping ground water from a well always causes (1) a decline in ground-water levels (heads; see Figure 7) at and near the well, and (2) a diversion to the pumping well of ground water that was moving slowly to its natural, possibly distant, area of discharge.** Pumping of a single well typically has a local effect on the ground-water-flow system. Pumping of many wells (sometimes hundreds or thousands of wells) in large areas can have regionally significant effects on ground-water systems.

- **Ground-water heads respond to pumping to markedly different degrees in unconfined and confined aquifers.** Pumping the same quantity of water from wells in confined and in unconfined aquifers initially results in much larger declines in heads over much larger areas for the confined aquifers (see Box A). This is because less water is available from storage in confined aquifers compared to unconfined aquifers. At a later time, as the amount of water derived from storage decreases and the system approaches equilibrium, the response of the system no longer depends upon being confined or unconfined. The amount of head decline at equilibrium is a function of the transmitting properties of the aquifers and confining units, discharge rate of the well, and distance to ground-water-system boundaries. Many aquifers, such as the upper part of the deep flow subsystem shown in Figure 6, exhibit a response to pumping that is intermediate between a completely confined and a completely unconfined aquifer system.

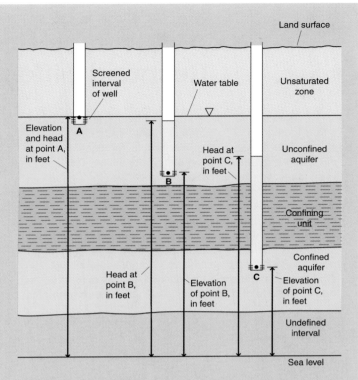

Figure 7. The concept of "hydraulic head" or "head" at a point in an aquifer.

Consider the elevations above sea level at points A and B in an unconfined aquifer and C in a confined aquifer. Now consider the addition of wells with short screened intervals at these three points. The vertical distance from the water level in each well to sea level is a measure of hydraulic head or head, referenced to a common datum at each point A, B, and C, respectively. Thus, head at a point in an aquifer is the sum of (a) the elevation of the point above a common datum, usually sea level, and (b) the height above the point of a column of static water in a well that is screened at the point. When we discuss declines or rises in ground-water levels in a particular aquifer in this report, we are referring to changes in head or water levels in wells that are screened or have an open interval in that aquifer.

11

Confined and Unconfined Aquifers Respond Differently to Pumping

The markedly different response of confined and unconfined aquifers to pumping (before the ground-water system returns to a new equilibrium) is demonstrated by calculations of drawdown resulting from a single pumping well in an idealized example of each type of aquifer (Figures A–1 and A–2). The numerical values used in the calculations are listed in Table A–1. Inspection of these values indicates that they are the same except for the storage coefficient S. Herein lies the key, which we discuss further in this section. To a hydrogeologist, the values in Table A–1 indicate a moderately permeable (K) and transmissive (T) aquifer, typical values of the storage coefficient S for confined and unconfined aquifers, and a high rate of continuous pumping (Q) for one year (t).

A mathematical solution was developed by Theis (1940) to calculate drawdowns caused by a single well in an aquifer of infinite extent where the only source of water is from storage. This solution was used to calculate drawdowns at the end of one year of pumping for the confined and unconfined aquifers defined by the values in Table A–1. These drawdowns are plotted on Figure A–3. Inspection of Figure A–3 shows that drawdowns in the confined aquifer are always larger than drawdowns in the unconfined aquifer, and that significant, or at least measurable, drawdowns occur at much larger distances from the pumping well in the confined aquifer. For example, at a distance of 10,000 feet (about 2 miles) from the pumping well, the drawdown in the unconfined

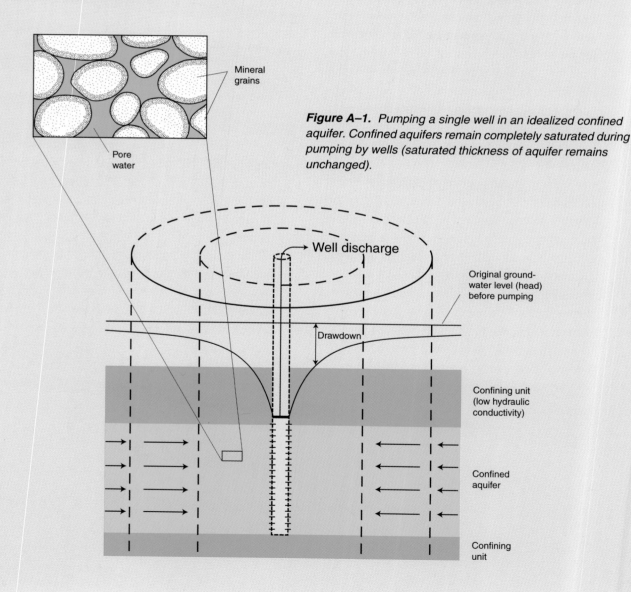

Figure A–1. Pumping a single well in an idealized confined aquifer. Confined aquifers remain completely saturated during pumping by wells (saturated thickness of aquifer remains unchanged).

Mineral grains

Pore water

Well discharge

Original ground-water level (head) before pumping

Drawdown

Confining unit (low hydraulic conductivity)

Confined aquifer

Confining unit

aquifer is too small to plot in Figure A–3, and the draw-down in the confined aquifer is about 10 feet. Furthermore, a measurable drawdown still occurs in the confined aquifer at a distance of 500,000 feet (about 95 miles) from the pumping well. Considering this information in a spatial sense, the cone of depression (Figure A–4) associated with the pumping well in the confined aquifer is deeper and much more areally extensive compared to the cone of depression in the unconfined aquifer. In fact, the total volume of the cone of depression in the confined aquifer is about 2,000 times larger than the total volume of the cone of depression in the uncon-fined aquifer for this example of a hypothetical infinite aquifer.

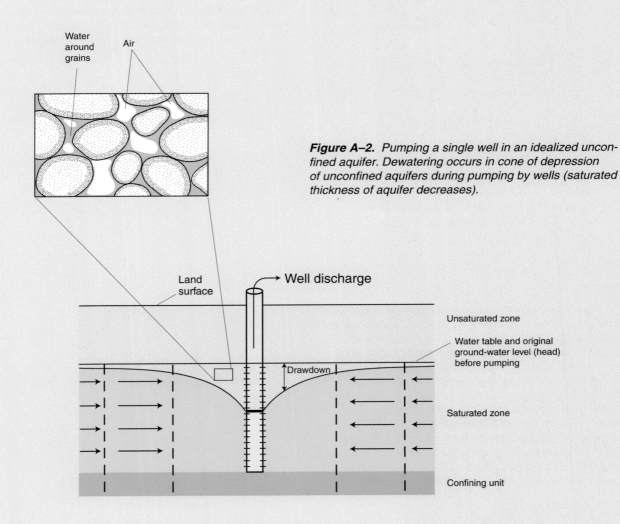

Figure A–2. *Pumping a single well in an idealized uncon-fined aquifer. Dewatering occurs in cone of depression of unconfined aquifers during pumping by wells (saturated thickness of aquifer decreases).*

Table A–1. *Numerical values of parameters used to calculate drawdowns in ground-water levels in response to pumping in two idealized aquifers, one confined and one unconfined*

Parameter	Confined aquifer	Unconfined aquifer
Hydraulic conductivity, K	100 feet per day	100 feet per day
Aquifer thickness, b	100 feet	100 feet
Transmissivity, T	10,000 feet squared per day	10,000 feet squared per day
Storage coefficient, S	0.0001	0.2
Duration of pumping, t	365 days	365 days
Rate of pumping, Q	192,500 cubic feet per day (1,000 gallons per minute)	192,500 cubic feet per day (1,000 gallons per minute)

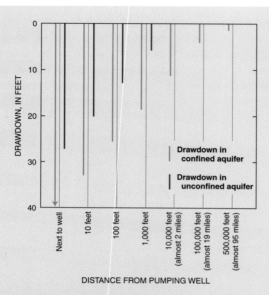

Figure A–3. Comparison of drawdowns after 1 year at selected distances from single wells that are pumped at the same rate in an idealized confined aquifer and an idealized unconfined aquifer. Note that the distances on the x-axis are not constant or to scale.

allows the water to expand slightly and causes a slight compression of the solid skeleton of earth material in the aquifer. The volume of water released from storage per unit volume of earth material in the cone of depression in a confined aquifer is small compared to the volume of water released by dewatering of the earth materials in an unconfined aquifer. The difference in how the two types of aquifers respond to pumping is reflected in the large numerical difference for values of the storage coefficient S in Table A–1.

The idealized aquifers and associated calculations of aquifer response to pumping discussed here represent ideal end members of a continuum; that is, the response of many real aquifers lies somewhere between the responses in these idealized examples.

The large differences in drawdowns and related volumes of the cone of depression in the two types of aquifers relate directly to how the two types of aquifers respond to pumping. In unconfined aquifers (Figure A–2) dewatering of the formerly saturated space between grains or in cracks or solution holes takes place. This dewatering results in significant volumes of water being released from storage per unit volume of earth material in the cone of depression. On the other hand, in confined aquifers (Figure A–1) the entire thickness of the aquifer remains saturated during pumping. However, pumping causes a decrease in head and an accompanying decrease in water pressure in the aquifer within the cone of depression. This decrease in water pressure

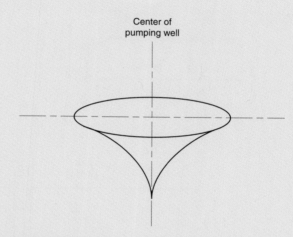

Figure A–4. The cone of depression associated with a pumping well in a homogeneous aquifer.

GROUND-WATER DEVELOPMENT, SUSTAINABILITY, AND WATER BUDGETS

A ground-water system consists of a mass of water flowing through the pores or cracks below the Earth's surface. This mass of water is in motion. Water is constantly added to the system by recharge from precipitation, and water is constantly leaving the system as discharge to surface water and as evapotranspiration. Each ground-water system is unique in that the source and amount of water flowing through the system is dependent upon external factors such as rate of precipitation, location of streams and other surface-water bodies, and rate of evapotranspiration. The one common factor for all ground-water systems, however, is that the total amount of water entering, leaving, and being stored in the system must be conserved. An accounting of all the inflows, outflows, and changes in storage is called a water budget.

Human activities, such as ground-water withdrawals and irrigation, change the natural flow patterns, and these changes must be accounted for in the calculation of the water budget. Because any water that is used must come from somewhere, human activities affect the amount and rate of movement of water in the system, entering the system, and leaving the system.

Some hydrologists believe that a predevelopment water budget for a ground-water system (that is, a water budget for the natural conditions before humans used the water) can be used to calculate the amount of water available for consumption (or the safe yield). In this case, the development of a ground-water system is considered to be "safe" if the rate of ground-water withdrawal does not exceed the rate of natural recharge. This concept has been referred to as the "Water-Budget Myth" (Bredehoeft and others, 1982). It is a myth because it is an oversimplification of the information that is needed to understand the effects of developing a ground-water system. As human activities change the system, the components of the water budget (inflows, outflows, and changes in storage) also will change and must be accounted for in any management decision. Understanding water budgets and how they change in response to human activities is an important aspect of ground-water hydrology; however, as we shall see, a predevelopment water budget by itself is of limited value in determining the amount of ground water that can be withdrawn on a sustained basis.

Some hydrologists believe that a predevelopment water budget for a ground-water system (that is, a water budget for the natural conditions before humans used the water) can be used to calculate the amount of water available for consumption (or the safe yield). This concept has been referred to as the "Water-Budget Myth."

Ground-Water Budgets

Under predevelopment conditions, the ground-water system is in long-term equilibrium. That is, averaged over some period of time, the amount of water entering or recharging the system is approximately equal to the amount of water leaving or discharging from the system. Because the system is in equilibrium, the quantity of water stored in the system is constant or varies about some average condition in response to annual or longer-term climatic variations. This predevelopment water budget is shown schematically in Figure 8A.

We also can write an equation that describes the water budget of the predevelopment system as:

Recharge (water entering) =
Discharge (water leaving)

The water leaving often is discharged to streams and rivers and is called base flow. The possible inflows (recharge) and outflows (discharge) of a ground-water system under natural (equilibrium) conditions are listed in Table 1.

Table 1. Possible sources of water entering and leaving a ground-water system under natural conditions

Inflow (recharge)	Outflow (discharge)
1. Areal recharge from precipitation that percolates through the unsaturated zone to the water table.	1. Discharge to streams, lakes, wetlands, saltwater bodies (bays, estuaries, or oceans), and springs.
2. Recharge from losing streams, lakes, and wetlands.	2. Ground-water evapotranspiration.

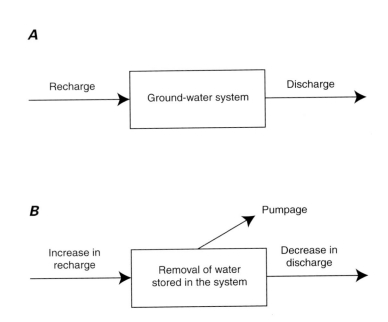

Figure 8. *Diagrams illustrating water budgets for a ground-water system for predevelopment and development conditions.*

(A) Predevelopment water-budget diagram illustrating that inflow equals outflow. (B) Water-budget diagram showing changes in flow for a ground-water system being pumped. The sources of water for the pumpage are changes in recharge, discharge, and the amount of water stored. The initial predevelopment values do not directly enter the budget calculation.

Humans change the natural or predevelopment flow system by withdrawing (pumping) water for use, changing recharge patterns by irrigation and urban development, changing the type of vegetation, and other activities. Focusing our attention on the effects of withdrawing ground water, we can conclude that the source of water for pumpage must be supplied by (1) more water entering the ground-water system (increased recharge), (2) less water leaving the system (decreased discharge), (3) removal of water that was stored in the system, or some combination of these three.

This statement, illustrated in Figure 8B, can be written in terms of rates (or volumes over a specified period of time) as:

Pumpage = Increased recharge + Water removed from storage + Decreased discharge.

It is the changes in the system that allow water to be withdrawn. That is, the water pumped must come from some change of flows and from removal of water stored in the predevelopment system (Theis, 1940; Lohman, 1972). The predevelopment water budget does not provide information on where the water will come from to supply the amount withdrawn. Furthermore, the predevelopment water budget only indirectly provides information on the amount of water perennially available, in that it can only indicate the magnitude of the original discharge that can be decreased (captured) under possible, usually extreme, development alternatives at possible significant expense to the environment.

The source of water for pumpage is supplied by (1) more water entering the ground-water system (increased recharge), (2) less water leaving the system (decreased discharge), (3) removal of water that was stored in the system, or some combination of these three.

Regardless of the amount of water withdrawn, the system will undergo some drawdown in water levels in pumping wells to induce the flow of water to these wells, which means that some water initially is removed from storage. Thus, the ground-water system serves as both a water reservoir and a water-distribution system. For most ground-water systems, the change in storage in response to pumping is a transient phenomenon that occurs as the system readjusts to the pumping stress. The relative contributions of changes in storage, changes in recharge, and changes in discharge evolve with time. The initial response to withdrawal of water is changes in storage. If the system can come to a new equilibrium, the changes in storage will stop and inflows will again balance outflows:

$$\text{Pumpage} = \text{Increased recharge} + \text{Decreased discharge}$$

Thus, the long-term source of water to discharging wells is typically a change in the amount of water entering or leaving the system. How much ground water is available for use depends upon how these changes in inflow and outflow affect the surrounding environment and what the public defines as undesirable effects on the environment.

In determining the effects of pumping and the amount of water available for use, it is critical to recognize that not all the water pumped is necessarily consumed. For example, not all the water pumped for irrigation is consumed by evapotranspiration. Some of the water returns to the ground-water system as infiltration (irrigation return flow). Most other uses of ground water are similar in that some of the water pumped is not consumed but is returned to the system. Thus, it is important to differentiate between the amount of water pumped and the amount of water consumed when estimating water availability and developing sustainable management strategies.

The possibilities of severe, long-term droughts and climate change also should be considered (see Box B). Long-term droughts, which virtually always result in reduced ground-water recharge, may be viewed as a natural stress on a ground-water system that in many ways has effects similar to ground-water withdrawals—namely, reductions in ground-water storage and accompanying reductions in ground-water discharge to streams and other surface-water bodies. Because a climate stress on the hydrologic system is added to the existing or projected human-derived stress, droughts represent extreme hydrologic conditions that should be evaluated in any long-term management plan.

Consideration of climate can be a key, but underemphasized, factor in ensuring the sustainability and proper management of ground-water resources.

Droughts, Climate Change, and Ground-Water Sustainability

The term "drought" has different meanings to different people, depending on how a water deficiency affects them. Droughts have been classified into different types such as meteorological drought (lack of precipitation), agricultural drought (lack of soil moisture), or hydrologic drought (reduced streamflow or ground-water levels). It is not unusual for a given period of water deficiency to represent a more severe drought of one type than another type. For example, a prolonged dry period during the summer may substantially lower the yield of crops due to a shortage of soil moisture in the plant root zone but have little effect on ground-water storage replenished the previous spring. On the other hand, a prolonged dry period when maximum recharge normally occurs can lower ground-water levels to the point at which shallow wells go dry.

Ground-water systems are a possible backup source of water during periods of drought. If ground-water storage is large and the effects of existing ground-water development are minimal, droughts may have limited, if any, effect on the long-term sustainability of aquifer systems from a storage perspective. In contrast, where ground-water storage and heads have been substantially reduced by withdrawals of ground water before a drought occurs, ground water may be less useful as a source of water to help communities and others cope with droughts. Furthermore, previous ground-water withdrawals can cause water levels and flows in lakes, streams, and other water bodies during droughts to be below limits that would have occurred in the absence of ground-water development. Likewise, reduced freshwater discharges to coastal areas during droughts may cause seawater to move beyond previous landward limits, or reduced heads in aquifers may cause renewed land subsidence (Figure B–1).

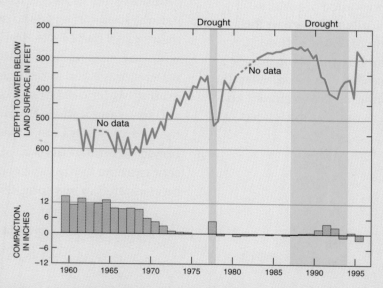

Figure B–1. Effects of drought on ground-water levels and associated subsidence in the San Joaquin Valley of California. (Modified from Galloway and Riley, in press; and Swanson, 1998.)

The San Joaquin Valley is a major agricultural area that produces a large fraction of the fruits, nuts, and vegetables in the United States. Ground-water withdrawals during the 1930's to early 1960's caused water-level declines of tens to hundreds of feet in much of the valley. The water-level declines resulted in compaction of the alluvial deposits and extensive land subsidence. Subsidence in excess of 1 foot has affected more than 5,200 square miles in the San Joaquin Valley, representing perhaps the largest anthropogenic change in land-surface elevation in the world. Importation of surface water, beginning in the 1960's, led to a decrease in ground-water withdrawals, which in turn led to rising ground-water levels and at least a temporary end to further subsidence. During severe droughts in 1976–77 and 1987–93, deliveries of imported water were decreased. More ground water was pumped to meet water demands, resulting in a decline in the water table and a renewal of compaction and land subsidence.

A common response to droughts is to drill more wells. Increased use of ground water may continue after a drought because installation of wells and the infrastructure for delivery of ground water can be a considerable investment. Thus, a drought may lead to a permanent, unanticipated change in the level of ground-water development. Use of ground-water resources for mitigating the effects of droughts is likely to be most effective with advance planning for that purpose.

Ground-water systems tend to respond much more slowly to short-term variability in climate conditions than do surface-water systems. As a result, assessments of ground-water resources and related model simulations commonly are based on average conditions, such as average annual recharge or average annual discharge to streams. This use of average conditions may underestimate the importance of droughts.

The effect of potential long-term changes in climate, including changes in average conditions and in climate variability, also merits consideration. Climate change could affect ground-water sustainability in several ways, including (1) changes in ground-water recharge resulting from changes in average precipitation and temperature or in the seasonal distribution of precipitation, (2) more severe and longer lasting droughts, (3) changes in evapotranspiration resulting from changes in vegetation, and (4) possible increased demands for ground water as a backup source of water supply. Surficial aquifers, which supply much of the flow to streams, lakes, wetlands, and springs, are likely to be the part of the ground-water system most sensitive to climate change; yet, limited attention has been directed at determining the possible effects of climate change on shallow aquifers and their interaction with surface water.

In summary, consideration of climate can be a key, but underemphasized, factor in ensuring the sustainability and proper management of ground-water resources. As increasing attention is placed on the interactions of ground water with land and surface-water resources, concerns about the effects of droughts, other aspects of climate variability, and the potential effects of climate change are likely to increase.

During the final preparation of this report in the summer of 1999, much of the Eastern United States was experiencing a severe drought, causing shallow wells to go dry in many areas. A few inches of rainfall in late August returned lawns to a healthy green color in this part of rural Virginia (note wellhead near home). However, these storms had little effect on ground-water levels because of the large cumulative moisture deficit in the unsaturated zone. Up to 6 inches or more of sustained precipitation from Tropical Storm Dennis over Labor Day weekend had a more substantial effect on ground-water levels, but parts of the Eastern United States unaffected by the tropical storm remained dry. In mid-September, Hurricane Floyd brought additional rain to the region. The drought intensified concerns about development of ground-water resources and the effects of possible interference between pumping wells, particularly in rapidly developing parts of the Piedmont where some of the fastest growing counties in the Nation are located.

Hypothetical Examples of How Ground-Water Systems Change in Response to Pumping

Consider a ground-water system in which the only natural source of inflow is areal recharge from precipitation. The amount of inflow is thus relatively fixed. Further consider that the primary sources of any water pumped from this ground-water system are removal from storage, decreased discharge to streams, and decreased transpiration by plants rooted near the water table.

If the above-described ground-water system can come to a new equilibrium after a period of removing water from storage, the amount of water consumed is balanced by less water flowing to surface-water bodies, and perhaps, less water available for transpiration by vegetation as the water table declines. If the consumptive use is so large that a new equilibrium cannot be achieved, water would continue to be removed from storage. In either case, less water will be available to surface-water users and the ecological resources dependent on streamflow. Depending upon the location of the water withdrawals, the headwaters of streams may begin to go dry. If the vegetation receives less water, the vegetative character of the area also might change. These various effects illustrate how the societal issue of what constitutes an undesired result enters into the determination of ground-water sustainability. The tradeoff between water for consumption and the effects of withdrawals on the environment often become the driving force in determining a good management scheme.

In most situations, withdrawals from ground-water systems are derived primarily from decreased ground-water discharge and decreased ground-water storage. These sources of water were thus emphasized in the previous example. Two special situations in which increased recharge can occur in response to ground-water withdrawals are noted here.

Pumping ground water can increase recharge by inducing flow from a stream into the ground-water system. When streams flowing across ground-water systems originate in areas outside these systems, the source of water being discharged by pumpage can be supplied in part by streamflow that originates upstream from the ground-water basin. In this case, the predevelopment water budget of the ground-water system does not account for a source of water outside the ground-water system that is potentially available as recharge from the stream.

Another potential source of increased recharge is the capture of recharge that was originally rejected because water levels were at or near land surface. As the water table declines in response to pumping, a storage capacity for infiltration of water becomes available in the unsaturated zone. As a result, some water that previously was rejected as surface runoff can recharge the aquifer and cause a net increase in recharge. This source of water to pumping wells is usually negligible, however, compared to other sources.

In summary, estimation of the amount of ground water that is available for use requires consideration of two key elements. First, the use of ground water and surface water must be evaluated together on a systemwide basis. This evaluation includes the amount of water available from changes in ground-water recharge, from changes in ground-water discharge, and from changes in storage for different levels of water consumption. Second, because any use of ground water changes the subsurface and surface environment (that is, the water must come from somewhere), the public should determine the tradeoff between ground-water use and changes to the environment and set a threshold at which the level of change becomes undesirable. This threshold can then be used in conjunction with a systemwide analysis of the ground-water and surface-water resources to determine appropriate limits for consumptive use.

Systemwide hydrologic analyses typically use simulations (that is, computer models) to aid in estimating water availability and the effects of extracting water on the ground-water and surface-water system. Computer models attempt to reproduce the most important features of an actual system with a mathematical representation. If constructed correctly, the model represents the complex relations among the inflows, outflows, changes in storage, movement of water in the system, and possibly other important features. As a mathematical representation of the system, the model can be used to estimate the response of the system to various development options and provide insight into appropriate management strategies. However, a computer model is a simplified representation of the actual system, and the judgment of water-management professionals is required to evaluate model simulation results and plan appropriate actions. We return to the use of models in the final chapter of this report, "Meeting the Challenges of Ground-Water Sustainability."

Because any use of ground water changes the subsurface and surface environment (that is, the water must come from somewhere), the public should determine the tradeoff between ground-water use and changes to the environment and set a threshold for what level of change becomes undesirable.

Field Examples of How Ground-Water Systems Change in Response to Pumping

LONG ISLAND, NEW YORK

Long Island is bounded on the north by Long Island Sound, on the east and south by the Atlantic Ocean, and on the west by New York Bay and the East River. Long Island is divided into four counties—Kings, Queens, Nassau, and Suffolk. The two western counties, Kings and Queens, are part of New York City.

Precipitation that infiltrates and percolates to the water table is Long Island's only natural source of freshwater because the ground-water system is bounded on the bottom by relatively imperme-able bedrock and on the sides by saline ground water or saline bays and the ocean (Figure 9). About one-half the precipitation becomes recharge to the ground-water system; the rest flows as surface runoff to streams or is lost through evapo-transpiration (Cohen and others, 1968). Much of the precipitation that reaches the uppermost unconfined aquifer moves laterally and discharges to streams and surrounding saltwater bodies; the remainder seeps downward to recharge the deeper aquifers. Water enters these deeper aquifers very slowly in areas where confining units are present but enters freely in other areas where confining units are absent. Water

in the deeper aquifers also moves seaward and eventually seeps into overlying aquifers. Predevel-opment water budgets for most of Nassau and Suffolk Counties on Long Island are shown in Figure 9.

Over the past three centuries, the island's ground water has been developed through three distinct phases. In the first, which began with the arrival of European settlers in the mid-17th century, virtually every house had its own shallow well, which tapped the uppermost unconsolidated geologic deposits, and also had its own cesspool, which returned wastewater to these same deposits. Because population was sparse, this mode of operation had little effect on the quantity and quality of shallow ground water. During the next two centuries, the population increased steadily, and, by the end of the 19th century, the individual wells in some areas had been abandoned in favor of shallow public-supply wells.

The second phase began with the rapid population growth and urban development that occurred during the first half of the 20th century. The high permeability of Long Island's deposits encouraged the widespread use of domestic wastewater-disposal systems, and the contamina-tion resulting from increased wastewater discharge led to the eventual abandonment of many domestic wells and shallow public-supply wells in favor of deeper, high-capacity wells. In general, pumping these deep wells had only a small effect on the quantity of shallow ground water and related surface-water systems because most of the water was returned to the ground-water reservoir through domestic wastewater-disposal systems.

OVERALL PREDEVELOPMENT WATER-BUDGET ANALYSIS

INFLOW TO LONG ISLAND HYDROLOGIC SYSTEM	CUBIC FEET PER SECOND
1. Precipitation	2,475
OUTFLOW FROM LONG ISLAND HYDROLOGIC SYSTEM	
2. Evapotranspiration of precipitation	1,175
3. Ground-water discharge to sea	725
4. Streamflow discharge to sea	525
5. Evapotranspiration of ground water	25
6. Spring flow	25
Total outflow	2,475

GROUND-WATER PREDEVELOPMENT WATER-BUDGET ANALYSIS

INFLOW TO LONG ISLAND GROUND-WATER SYSTEM	CUBIC FEET PER SECOND
7. Ground-water recharge	1,275
OUTFLOW FROM LONG ISLAND GROUND-WATER SYSTEM	
8. Ground-water discharge to streams	500
9. Ground-water discharge to sea	725
10. Evapotranspiration of ground water	25
11. Spring flow	25
Total outflow	1,275

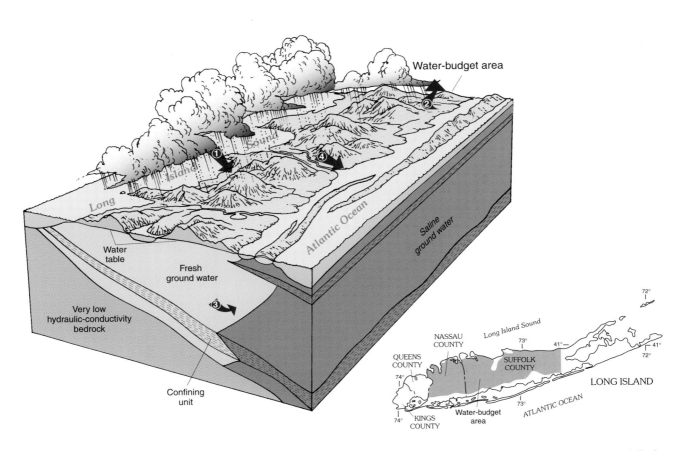

Figure 9. *Ground-water budget for part of Nassau and Suffolk Counties, Long Island, New York. (Modified from Cohen and others, 1968.)*

Block diagram of Long Island, New York, and tables listing the overall water budget and ground-water budget under predevelopment conditions. Both water budgets assume equilibrium conditions with little or no change in storage.

The third and present phase of ground-water development on Long Island began in the early 1950's with the introduction of large-scale sewer systems in the more heavily populated areas. The purpose of the sewers was to prevent domestic wastewater from entering the aquifer system because contaminants from this source were being detected in deep public-supply wells. Even though the sewers protect the aquifers from further contamination, they also prevent the replenishment (recharge) that the wastewater had provided to the ground-water reservoir through the domestic wastewater-disposal systems. The wastewater is now diverted to sewage-treatment plants, whose effluent is discharged to the bays and oceans. The decrease in recharge has caused the water table in the sewered areas to be substantially lowered, the base flow of streams to be reduced or eliminated, and the length of perennial streams to be decreased.

In Nassau and Suffolk Counties, about 200 cubic feet per second of wastewater (ground water that has been pumped and used) was discharged in 1985 by the three major sewer districts to the surrounding saltwater bodies (Spinello and Simmons, 1992). As previously noted, the only source of freshwater to the system is precipitation. Therefore, the water required to balance the loss from the ground-water system must come primarily from decreases in ground-water discharge to streams and to surrounding saltwater bodies. Capture of ground-water evapotranspiration, spring flow, and some surface runoff are also possible, but each of these sources is limited to a maximum of approximately 25 cubic feet per second (Figure 9). As the flow to the streams decreases, the headwaters of the streams dry up and the streams become shorter. As the discharge of ground water to surrounding saltwater bodies decreases, saline ground water moves landward as saltwater intrusion. Thus, this case is an example in which the determination of sustainable yields cannot be based solely on predevelopment water budgets. The specific response of the ground-water system to development must be taken into account in determining the appropriate limits to set on ground-water use.

HIGH PLAINS AQUIFER

The High Plains is a 174,000-square-mile area of flat to gently rolling terrain that includes parts of Colorado, Kansas, Nebraska, New Mexico, Oklahoma, South Dakota, Texas, and Wyoming. The area is characterized by moderate precipitation but generally has a low natural recharge rate to the ground-water system. Unconsolidated alluvial deposits that form a water-table aquifer called the High Plains aquifer (consisting largely of the Ogallala aquifer) underlie the region. Irrigation water pumped from the aquifer has made the High Plains one of the Nation's most important agricultural areas.

During the late 1800's, settlers and speculators moved to the plains, and farming became the major activity in the area. The drought of the 1930's gave rise to the use of irrigation and improved farming practices in the High Plains (Gutentag and others, 1984). Around 1940, a rapid expansion in the use of ground water for irrigation began. In 1949, about 480 million cubic feet per day of ground water was used for irrigation. By 1980, the use had more than quadrupled to about 2,150 million cubic feet per day (U.S. Geological Survey, 1984). Subsequently, it declined to about 1,870 million cubic feet per day in 1990 (McGuire and Sharpe, 1997). Not all of the water pumped for irrigation is consumed as evapotranspiration by crops; some seeps back into the ground and recharges the aquifer. Nevertheless, this intense use of ground water has caused major water-level declines (Figure 10A) and decreased the saturated thickness of the aquifer significantly in some areas (Figure 10B). These changes are particularly evident in the central and southern parts of the High Plains.

The southern part of the High Plains aquifer in Texas and New Mexico slopes gently from west to east, cut off from external sources of water upstream and downstream by river-carved escarpments, as shown in Figure 11A. Thus, ground-water recharge is due almost exclusively to areal recharge from precipitation. Although precipitation in the area is 15 to 20 inches per year, only a fraction of an inch recharges the aquifer due to high evapotranspiration from the soil zone. During predevelopment conditions, discharge as seeps and springs along the eastern escarpment equaled recharge. Today, the magnitude of natural recharge and discharge is small compared to withdrawals for irrigation.

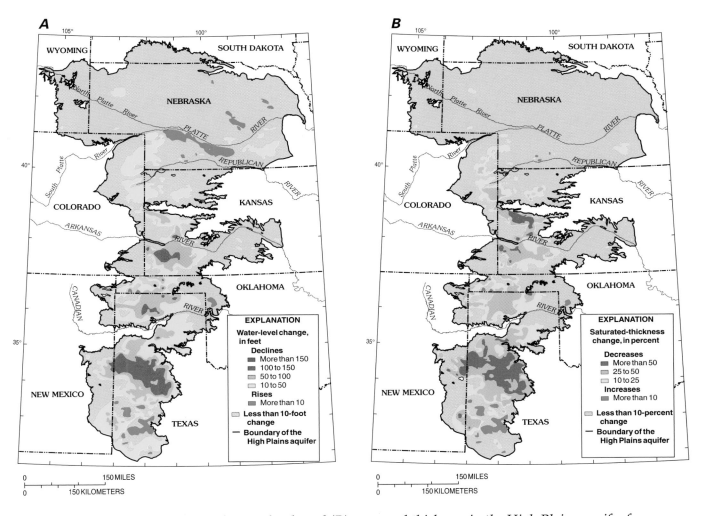

Figure 10. *Changes in (A) ground-water levels and (B) saturated thickness in the High Plains aquifer from predevelopment to 1997. (V.L. McGuire, U.S. Geological Survey, written commun., 1998.)*

Extensive pumping of ground water for irrigation has led to ground-water-level declines in excess of 100 feet in parts of the High Plains aquifer in Kansas, New Mexico, Oklahoma, and Texas. These large water-level declines have led to reductions in saturated thickness of the aquifer exceeding 50 percent of the predevelopment saturated thickness in some areas. Lower ground-water levels cause increases in pumping lifts. Decreases in saturated thickness result in declining well yields. Surface-water irrigation has resulted in water-level rises in some parts of the aquifer system, such as along the Platte River in Nebraska.

The predevelopment water budget and a water budget for average developed conditions in the southern High Plains aquifer during 1960–80 are shown in Figure 11B. Comparison of these water budgets shows that, due to irrigation return flow, recharge to the High Plains aquifer increased more than twentyfold from an estimated 24 million cubic feet per day during predevelopment to about 510 million cubic feet per day during 1960–80. This increase in recharge (about 486 million cubic feet per day) together with the decrease in storage (about 330 million cubic feet per day) accounts for over 98 percent of the total pumpage (about 830 million cubic feet per day). Less than 2 percent of the pumpage is accounted for by decreases in natural discharge (about 14 million cubic feet per day).

A long delay between pumping and its effects on natural discharge from the High Plains aquifer is caused by the large distance between many of the pumping wells and the location of the springs and seeps that discharge from the ground-water system. The southern High Plains is perhaps the best known example of significant, long-term nonequilibrium for a regional ground-water system in the United States. That is, water levels continue to decline without reaching a new balance (equilibrium) between recharge to and discharge from the ground-water system.

Figure 11. The effects of ground-water withdrawals on the southern High Plains aquifer.

Schematic cross section (A) of the southern High Plains aquifer illustrating that ground-water withdrawal in the middle of the southern High Plains aquifer has a negligible short-term effect on the discharge at the boundaries of the aquifer. (Modified from Lohman, 1972.) (B) Water budgets of the southern High Plains aquifer (all flows in million cubic feet per day) before development and during development. (Modified from Johnston, 1989; data from Luckey and others, 1986).

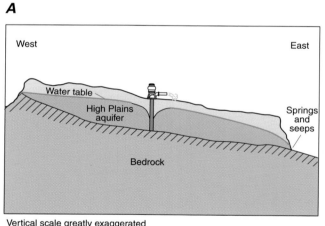

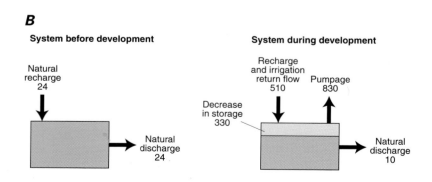

The preceding two field examples illustrate some of the complexities associated with the use of water budgets to determine the development potential of a ground-water system. Knowledge of the sources and discharges of water to and from the system and how they change with continuing development is needed to understand the response of ground-water systems to development, as well as to aid in determining appropriate management strategies and future use of the resource.

The examples discussed here and those in the following chapters illustrate several of the principles summarized by Bredehoeft and others (1982) in their article on the "water-budget myth" and earlier by Theis (1940):

- Some ground water must be removed from storage before the system can be brought into equilibrium.

- The time that is required to bring a hydrologic system into equilibrium depends on the rate at which the discharge can be captured.

- The rate at which discharge can be captured is a function of the characteristics of the aquifer system and the placement of pumping wells.

- Equilibrium is reached only when pumping is balanced by capture. In many circumstances, the dynamics of the ground-water system are such that long periods of time are necessary before even an approximate equilibrium condition can be reached.

In the next three chapters we discuss in more detail the effects of ground-water development on ground-water discharge to and recharge from surface-water bodies, the effects of ground-water development on ground-water storage, and water-quality factors affecting ground-water sustainability.

EFFECTS OF GROUND-WATER DEVELOPMENT ON GROUND-WATER FLOW TO AND FROM SURFACE-WATER BODIES

As development of land and water resources intensifies, it is increasingly apparent that development of either ground water or surface water affects the other (Winter and others, 1998). Some particular aspects of the interaction of ground water and surface water that affect the sustainable development of ground-water systems are discussed below for various types of surface-water features.

As development of land and water resources intensifies, it is increasingly apparent that development of either ground water or surface water affects the other.

Streams

Streams either gain water from inflow of ground water (gaining stream; Figure 12*A*) or lose water by outflow to ground water (losing stream; Figure 12*B*). Many streams do both, gaining in some reaches and losing in other reaches. Furthermore, the flow directions between ground water and surface water can change seasonally as the altitude of the ground-water table changes with respect to the stream-surface altitude or can change over shorter timeframes when rises in stream surfaces during storms cause recharge to the streambank. Under natural conditions, ground water makes some contribution to streamflow in most physiographic and climatic settings. Thus, even in settings where streams are primarily losing water to ground water, certain reaches may receive ground-water inflow during some seasons.

Losing streams can be connected to the ground-water system by a continuous saturated zone (Figure 12*B*) or can be disconnected from the ground-water system by an unsaturated zone (Figure 12*C*). An important feature of streams that are disconnected from ground water is that pumping of ground water near the stream does not affect the flow of the stream near the pumped well.

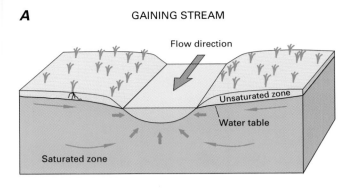

A GAINING STREAM

Flow direction

Unsaturated zone

Water table

Saturated zone

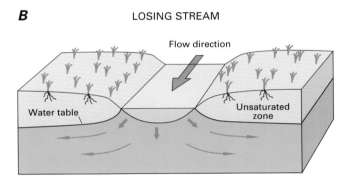

B LOSING STREAM

Flow direction

Water table

Unsaturated zone

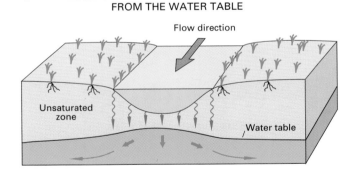

C LOSING STREAM THAT IS DISCONNECTED
FROM THE WATER TABLE

Flow direction

Unsaturated zone

Water table

*Figure 12. Interaction of streams and ground water.
(Modified from Winter and others, 1998.)*

*Gaining streams (A) receive water from the
ground-water system, whereas losing streams (B)
lose water to the ground-water system. For ground
water to discharge to a stream channel, the altitude of
the water table in the vicinity of the stream must be
higher than the altitude of the stream-water surface.
Conversely, for surface water to seep to ground water,
the altitude of the water table in the vicinity of the
stream must be lower than the altitude of the stream
surface. Some losing streams (C) are separated from
the saturated ground-water system by an unsaturated zone.*

A pumping well can change the quantity and
direction of flow between an aquifer and stream in
response to different rates of pumping. Figure 13
illustrates a simple case in which equilibrium is
attained for a hypothetical stream-aquifer system
and a single pumping well. The adjustments
to pumping of an actual hydrologic system may
take place over many years, depending upon the
physical characteristics of the aquifer, degree of
hydraulic connection between the stream and
aquifer, and locations and pumping history of
wells. Reductions of streamflow as a result of
ground-water pumping are likely to be of greatest
concern during periods of low flow, particularly
when the reliability of surface-water supplies is
threatened during droughts.

At the start of pumping, 100 percent of the
water supplied to a well comes from ground-water
storage. Over time, the dominant source of water
to a well, particularly wells that are completed in
an unconfined aquifer, commonly changes from
ground-water storage to surface water. The
surface-water source for purposes of discussion
here is a stream, but it may be another surface-
water body such as a lake or wetland. The source
of water to a well from a stream can be either
decreased discharge to the stream or increased
recharge from the stream to the ground-water
system. The streamflow reduction in either case
is referred to as streamflow capture.

In the long term, the cumulative streamflow capture for many ground-water systems
can approach the quantity of water pumped
from the ground-water system. This is illustrated
in Figure 14, which shows the time-varying
percentage of ground-water pumpage derived
from ground-water storage and the percentage
derived from streamflow capture for the hypothetical stream-aquifer system shown in Figure 13. The
time for the change from the dominance of withdrawal from ground-water storage to the dominance of streamflow capture can range from weeks
to years to decades or longer.

31

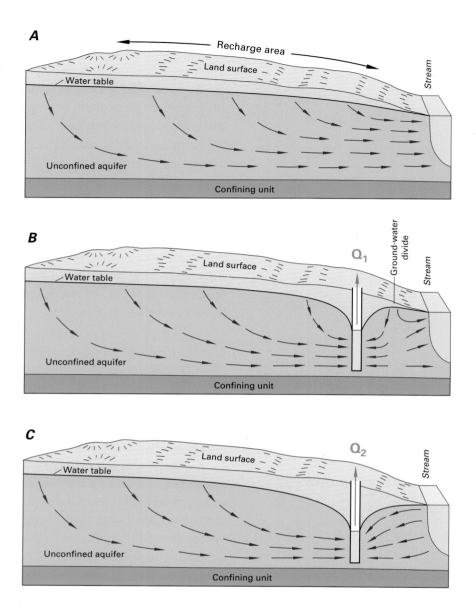

Figure 13. *Effects of pumping from a hypothetical ground-water system that discharges to a stream. (Modified from Heath, 1983.)*

Under natural conditions (A), recharge at the water table is equal to ground-water discharge to the stream. Assume a well is installed and is pumped continuously at a rate, Q_1, as in (B). After a new state of dynamic equilibrium is achieved, inflow to the ground-water system from recharge will equal outflow to the stream plus the withdrawal from the well. In this new equilibrium, some of the ground water that would have discharged to the stream is intercepted by the well, and a ground-water divide, which is a line separating directions of flow, is established locally between the well and the stream. If the well is pumped at a higher rate, Q_2, a different equilibrium is reached, as shown in (C). Under this condition, the ground-water divide between the well and the stream is no longer present, and withdrawals from the well induce movement of water from the stream into the aquifer. Thus, pumping reverses the hydrologic condition of the stream in this reach from ground-water discharge to ground-water recharge. Note that in the hydrologic system depicted in (A) and (B), the quality of the stream water generally will have little effect on the quality of ground water. In the case of the well pumping at the higher rate in (C), however, the quality of the stream water can affect the quality of ground water between the well and the stream, as well as the quality of the water withdrawn from the well. Although a stream is used in this example, the general concepts apply to all surface-water bodies, including lakes, reservoirs, wetlands, and estuaries.

Most ground-water development is much more complex than implied in Figure 13; for example, it may comprise many wells pumping from an aquifer at varying pumping rates and at different locations within the ground-water-flow system. Computer models commonly are needed to evaluate the time scale and time-varying response of surface-water bodies to such complex patterns of ground-water development. From a sustainability perspective, the key point is that pumping decisions today will affect surface-water availability; however, these effects may not be fully realized for many years.

The eventual reduction in surface-water supply as a result of ground-water development complicates the administration of water rights. Traditionally, water laws did not recognize the physical connection of ground water and surface water. Today, in parts of the Western United States, ground-water development and use are restricted because of their effects on surface-water rights. Accounting for the effects of ground-water development on surface-water rights can be difficult. For example, in the case of water withdrawn to irrigate a field, some of the water will be lost from the local hydrologic system due to evaporation and use by crops, while some may percolate to the ground-water system and ultimately be returned to the stream. Related questions that arise include: how much surface water will be captured, which surface-water bodies will be affected, and over what period will the effects occur? Some of these issues are illustrated further in Box C.

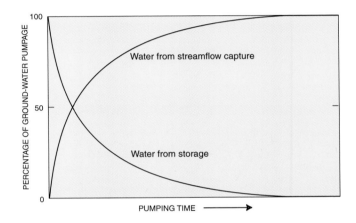

Figure 14. *The principal source of water to a well can change with time from ground-water storage to capture of streamflow.*

The percentage of ground-water pumpage derived from ground-water storage and capture of streamflow (decrease in ground-water discharge to the stream or increase in ground-water recharge from the stream) is shown as a function of time for the hypothetical stream-aquifer system shown in Figure 13. A constant pumping rate of the well is assumed. For this simple system, water derived from storage plus streamflow capture must equal 100 percent. The time scale of the curves shown depends on the hydraulic characteristics of the aquifer and the distance of the well from the stream.

Ground-water pumping can affect not only water supply for human consumption but also the maintenance of instream-flow requirements for fish habitat and other environmental needs. Long-term reductions in streamflow can affect vegetation along streams (riparian zones) that serve critical roles in maintaining wildlife habitat and in enhancing the quality of surface water. Pumping-induced changes in the flow direction to and from streams may affect temperature, oxygen levels, and nutrient concentrations in the stream, which may in turn affect aquatic life in the stream.

Perennial streams, springs, and wetlands in the Southwestern United States are highly valued as a source of water for humans and for the plant and animal species they support. Development of ground-water resources since the late 1800's has resulted in the elimination or alteration of many perennial stream reaches, wetlands, and associated riparian ecosystems. As an example, a 1942 photograph of a reach of the Santa Cruz River south of Tucson, Ariz., at Martinez Hill shows stands of mesquite and cottonwood trees along the river (left photograph). A replicate photograph of the same site in 1989 shows that the riparian trees have largely disappeared (right photograph). Data from two nearby wells indicate that the water table has declined more than 100 feet due to pumping, and this pumping appears to be the principal reason for the decrease in vegetation. (Photographs provided by Robert H. Webb, U.S. Geological Survey.)

In gaining and in losing streams, water and dissolved chemicals can move repeatedly over short distances between the stream and the shallow subsurface below the streambed. The resulting subsurface environments, which contain variable proportions of water from ground water and surface water, are referred to as hyporheic zones (see Figure 15). Hyporheic zones can be active sites for aquatic life. For example, the spawning success of fish may be greater where flow from the stream brings oxygen into contact with eggs that were deposited within the coarse bottom sediment or where stream temperatures are modulated by ground-water inflow. The effects of ground-water pumping on hyporheic zones and the resulting effects on aquatic life are not well known.

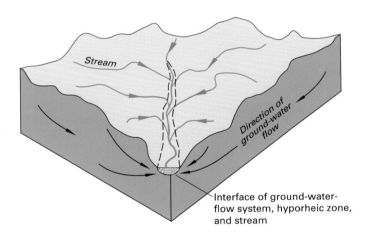

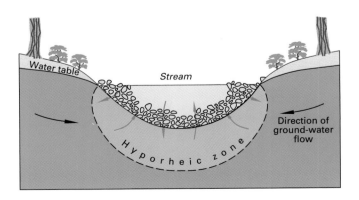

Figure 15. The dynamic interface between ground water and streams. (Modified from Winter and others, 1998.)

Streambeds are unique environments where ground water that drains much of the subsurface of landscapes interacts with surface water that drains much of the surface of landscapes. Mixing of surface water and ground water takes place in the hyporheic zone where microbial activity and chemical transformations commonly are enhanced.

35

Ground-Water/Surface-Water Interactions and Water-Resources Sustainability: Examples from the Northwestern United States

The effects of ground-water withdrawals on streamflow and spring discharge have become a major concern in parts of the Northwestern United States as continuing population growth increases the demand for water and pressures mount on the water resources to meet minimum instream-flow requirements for recreation and for fish and wildlife habitat. Examples from Washington and Idaho illustrate some of the complexities in how ground-water pumping affects surface-water resources.

PUGET SOUND LOWLAND, WASHINGTON

A numerical model of a hypothetical basin in the Puget Sound Lowland of western Washington was used by Morgan and Jones (1999) to illustrate the effects of ground-water withdrawals on discharge to streams and springs in small basins typical of the region. The hypothetical basin shown in Figure C–1 consists of glacial deposits and alluvial sediments along streams that overlie low hydraulic-conductivity bedrock (see Figure C–2).

The results of three simulations are used here to illustrate the effects of pumping on streamflow for each of three different locations of water withdrawal from a well: (1) the unconfined aquifer near stream segment A, (2) the

unconfined aquifer about 6,000 feet from stream segment A, and (3) a confined aquifer near stream segment A that is separated from the unconfined aquifer by about 25 feet of low-permeability till. The pumping well in simulation 1 and that in simulation 3 have the same land-surface location. The three simulations (simulations 1–3) are for steady-state conditions; that is, the ground-water system has reached dynamic equilibrium with the pumping from the well. For each simulation, the percentage of the ground water withdrawn that comes from capture of discharge to streams and their associated springs is shown in Table C–1 for five stream segments labeled A to E in Figure C–1.

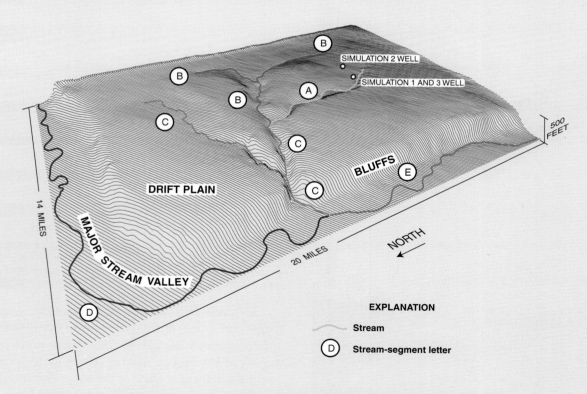

Figure C–1. Three-dimensional perspective view of a hypothetical basin typical of the Puget Sound Lowland showing topography, streams, and well locations for pumping simulations. (Modified from Morgan and Jones, 1999.)

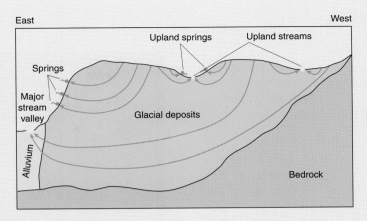

Figure C–2. *Simplified hydrogeologic section for basin shown in Figure C-1 showing generalized ground-water-flow paths under natural conditions. Confining units and their effect on the flow system are not shown. (Modified from Morgan and Jones, 1999.)*

At steady state, all of the ground-water withdrawal comes from capture of surface water for each of the three simulations. In looking at the distribution among stream reaches, virtually all of the captured water is from stream segment A when the water is pumped from a well in the unconfined aquifer near that stream segment (simulation 1). For a well located farther from stream segment A (simulation 2), most of the capture is still from stream segment A, but almost 25 percent of the capture is from the more distant stream segments B and E. Finally, if the water is withdrawn from the confined aquifer near stream segment A (simulation 3), about 50 percent of the capture comes from stream segment A, and the remainder comes from more distant stream segments.

The results illustrate that, because the effects of pumping propagate in all directions, several surface-water bodies can be affected by the water-level drawdowns caused by a pumping well. A well pumping from an unconfined aquifer will tend to capture most of its discharge from the nearest stream reaches. The presence of a confining layer between the well and the streams causes the cone of depression of the well to extend greater distances to capture the natural discharge required to offset pumping. Morgan and Jones (1999) demonstrated through additional simulations that, as the depth of the well and the number of confining layers increase, capture of discharge to streams and springs is distributed over increasingly larger areas.

Table C–1. *Streamflow capture along five stream segments for three pumping simulations: (1) pumping from well in unconfined aquifer near stream segment A, (2) pumping from well in unconfined aquifer about 6,000 feet from stream segment A, and (3) pumping from well in a confined aquifer near stream segment A*

	Streamflow capture along stream segment as percentage of pumpage		
Stream segment	**Simulation 1**	**Simulation 2***	**Simulation 3**
A	97	70	51
B	<1	12	13
C	<1	<1	5
D	<1	3	5
E	1	12	26

*Sum of percentages for simulation 2 is less than 100 due to rounding.

EASTERN SNAKE RIVER PLAIN, IDAHO

The previous example illustrates how capture of surface water might be distributed over a basin after equilibrium of the ground-water system has occurred. Computer simulations of the Eastern Snake River Plain aquifer by Hubbell and others (1997) illustrate how the effects of pumping on streamflow might be distributed through time before the ground-water system reaches equilibrium.

Highly permeable basaltic rocks of the Eastern Snake River Plain in Idaho provide conduits for rapid recharge of precipitation and water from extensive irrigation. Ground-water flow in this basaltic aquifer is primarily from northeast to southwest, as shown in Figure C–3. The aquifer is connected to the Snake River and discharges to the river largely through major springs, such as Thousand Springs at the downstream end of the flow system.

Thousand Springs

The timing of the effects of pumping on spring discharge to the Thousand Springs reach and to the entire eastern Snake River were simulated for each of four potential well sites (sites A–D in Figure C–3). For simulations at sites A to C, pumping was simulated at a constant rate for 100 years. Figure C–4 shows the depletion of flow to the river as a percentage of pumpage during the 100-year simulation. The river losses from pumping at site A are 50 percent of the pumpage after 23 years and about 90 percent after 100 years. Slightly more than half of the river depletion caused by pumping at site A occurs along the Thousand Springs reach.

Pumping at site B, located much closer to the Thousand Springs reach, has almost 90 percent of the pumpage obtained from capture of spring flow after 10 years of pumping. Most of the losses are from the Thousand Springs reach; river flow in the other reaches is only slightly affected by pumping at site B.

Site C is more distant from the Snake River. Pumping at this location has little effect on flows to the river for more than 10 years; however, depletion continuously increases during the long period of continuous pumping. The river depletion after 100 years of pumping at site C is about 70 percent of the pumpage.

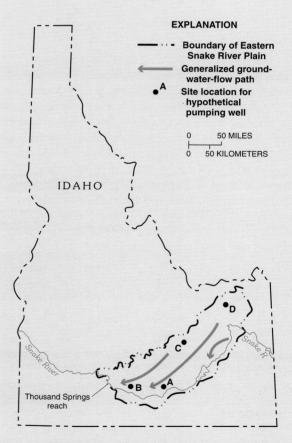

Figure C–3. Eastern Snake River Plain aquifer system. (Modified from Hubbell and others, 1997; reprinted with permission of the National Ground Water Association. Copyright 1997.)

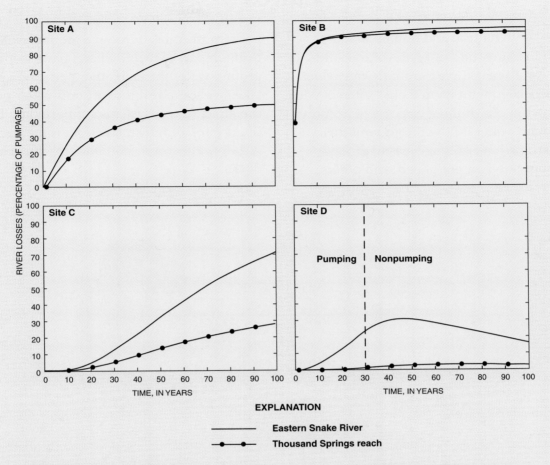

EXPLANATION

―――――― Eastern Snake River

●――●――● Thousand Springs reach

Figure C–4. *Simulated losses to the Snake River resulting from pumping at well sites A to D. (Modified from Hubbell and others, 1997; reprinted with permission of the National Ground Water Association. Copyright 1997.)*

The results of pumping at site D illustrate how surface-water depletion can continue long after pumping is discontinued at a well. These residual effects are demonstrated at site D by simulating continuous pumping for 30 years followed by a 70-year nonpumping period. Depletion of flow to the river increases for approximately 15 years after pumping at site D is discontinued. Depletion is still occurring 70 years after pumping ceases at a rate equivalent to 15 percent of the average pumping rate during the 30 years of pumping at site D.

The simulated results for sites A to D indicate that the location of a well relative to the ground-water-flow system has a significant effect on where changes in flow in the system take place and how long the system continues to adjust before equilibrium is reached. These results highlight the importance of taking transient response times of ground-water systems into account in long-term water-resources planning.

Lakes

Lakes, both natural and human made, are present in many different parts of the landscape and can have complex ground-water-flow systems associated with them. Lakes interact with ground water in one of three basic ways: some receive ground-water inflow throughout their entire bed; some have seepage loss to ground water throughout their entire bed; and others, perhaps most lakes, receive ground-water inflow through part of their bed and have seepage loss to ground water through other parts. Lowering of lake levels as a result of ground-water pumping can affect the ecosystems supported by the lake (Figure 16), diminish lakefront esthetics, and have negative effects on shoreline structures such as docks.

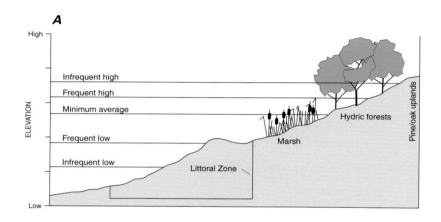

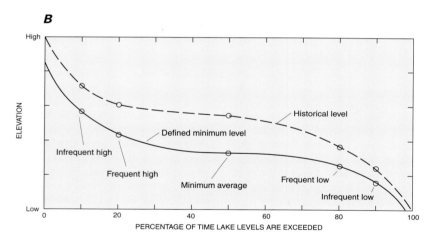

Figure 16. *Setting minimum water levels in Florida lakes. (Modified from McGrail and others, 1998.)*

As part of efforts to prevent significant undesirable environmental consequences from water-resources development, water-management agencies in Florida are defining minimum flows and water levels for priority surface waters and aquifers in the State. For lakes, the minimum flows and water levels describe a hydrologic regime that is less than the historical or optimal one but allows for prudent water use while protecting critical lake functions. As an example, five possible minimum water levels defined for a lake are shown in A. An elevation and a percentage of time the level is exceeded characterize each of these levels. The upper curve in B shows the percentage of the time that the lake is historically above each corresponding level. The goal is to ensure that water withdrawals and other water-resource management actions continue to allow the lake water levels to be at or above the minimum levels shown by the lower curve in B for the percentage of time shown.

Dock on Crooked Lake in central Florida in the 1970's.

The same dock in 1990.

As a result of very low topographic relief, high rainfall, and a karst terrain, the Florida landscape is characterized by numerous lakes and wetland areas. The underlying Floridan aquifer is one of the most extensive and productive aquifers in the world. Over the past two decades, lake levels declined and wetlands dried out in highly developed west-central Florida as a result of both extensive pumping and low precipitation during these years. Differentiating between the effects of the drought and pumping has been difficult. (Photographs courtesy of Florida Water Resources Journal, August, 1990 issue.)

The chemistry of ground water and the direction and magnitude of exchange with surface water significantly affect the input of dissolved chemicals to lakes. In fact, ground water can be the principal source of dissolved chemicals to a lake, even in cases where ground-water discharge is a small component of a lake's water budget. Changes in flow patterns to lakes as a result of pumping may alter the natural fluxes to lakes of key constituents such as nutrients and dissolved oxygen, in turn altering lake biota, their environment, and the interaction of both.

Wetlands

Wetlands are present wherever topography and climate favor the accumulation or retention of water on the landscape. Wetlands occur in widely diverse settings from coastal margins to flood plains to mountain valleys. Similar to streams and lakes, wetlands can receive ground-water inflow, recharge ground water, or do both. Wetlands are in many respects ground-water features.

Public and scientific views of wetlands have changed greatly over time. Only a few decades ago, wetlands generally were considered to be of little or no value. It is now recognized that wetlands have beneficial functions such as wildlife habitat, floodwater retention, protection of the land from erosion, shoreline protection in coastal areas, and water-quality improvement by filtering of contaminants.

The persistence, size, and function of wetlands are controlled by hydrologic processes (Carter, 1996). For example, the persistence of wetness for many wetlands is dependent on a relatively stable influx of ground water throughout changing seasonal and annual climatic cycles. Characterizing ground-water discharge to wetlands and its relation to environmental factors such as moisture content and chemistry in the root zone of wetland plants is a critical but difficult to characterize aspect of wetlands hydrology (Hunt and others, 1999).

Wetlands can be quite sensitive to the effects of ground-water pumping. Ground-water pumping can affect wetlands not only as a result of progressive lowering of the water table, but also by increased seasonal changes in the altitude of the water table. The amplitude and frequency of water-level fluctuations through changing seasons, commonly termed the hydroperiod, affect wetland characteristics such as the type of vegetation, nutrient cycling, and the type of invertebrates, fish, and bird species present. The effects on the wetland environment from changes to the hydroperiod may depend greatly on the time of year at which the effects occur. For example, lower than usual water levels during the nongrowing season might be expected to have less effect on the vegetation than similar water-level changes during the growing season. The effects of pumping on seasonal fluctuations in ground-water levels near wetlands add a new dimension to the usual concerns about sustainable development that typically focus on annual withdrawals (Bacchus, 1998).

Springs

Springs typically are present where the water table intersects the land surface. Springs serve as important sources of water to streams and other surface-water features, as well as being important cultural and esthetic features in themselves. The constant source of water at springs leads to the abundant growth of plants and, many times, to unique habitats. Ground-water development can lead to reductions in springflow, changes of springs from perennial to ephemeral, or elimination of springs altogether. Springs typically represent points on the landscape where ground-water-flow paths from different sources converge. Ground-water development may affect the amount of flow from these different sources to varying extents, thus affecting the resultant chemical composition of the spring water.

Comal Springs

The highly productive Edwards aquifer, the first aquifer to be designated as a sole source aquifer under the Safe Drinking Water Act, is the source of water for more than 1 million people in San Antonio, Texas, some military bases and small towns, and for south-central Texas farmers and ranchers. The aquifer also supplies water to sustain threatened and endangered species habitat associated with natural springs in the region and supplies surface water to users downstream from the major springs. These various uses are in direct competition with ground-water development and have created challenging issues of ground-water management in the region. (Photograph by Robert Morris, U.S. Geological Survey.)

Coastal Environments

Coastal areas are a highly dynamic interface between the continents and the ocean. The physical and chemical processes in these areas are quite complex and commonly are poorly understood. Historically, concern about ground water in coastal regions has focused on seawater intrusion into coastal aquifers, as discussed in a later chapter of this report. More recently, ground water has been recognized as an important contributor of nutrients and contaminants to coastal waters. Likewise, plant and wildlife communities adapted to particular environmental conditions in coastal areas can be affected by changes in the flow and quality of ground-water discharges to the marine environment.

In summary, we have seen that changes to surface-water bodies in response to ground-water pumping commonly are subtle and may occur over long periods of time. The cumulative effects of pumping can cause significant and unanticipated consequences when not properly considered in water-management plans. The types of water bodies that can be affected are highly varied, as are the potential effects.

EFFECTS OF GROUND-WATER DEVELOPMENT ON GROUND-WATER STORAGE

Previous chapters have discussed the "ground-water-flow system," including recharge and subsequent flow of ground water through the system to areas of discharge, primarily bodies of surface water. In this context, the ground-water-flow system functions as a conduit that transports water, sometimes over considerable distances (miles, tens of miles), from areas of recharge to areas of discharge. In this chapter, the focus changes from the dynamic aspect of the ground-water-flow system to another aspect—the fact that the flowing ground water in the system represents a large, sometimes huge, volume of water in storage. In this context, it is appropriate to change terminology from "ground-water-flow system" to "ground-water reservoir," which emphasizes the storage aspect of ground-water systems.

A key feature of some aquifers and ground-water systems is the large volume of ground water in storage, which allows the possibility of using aquifers for temporary storage, that is, managing inflow and outflow of ground water in storage in a manner similar to surface-water reservoirs.

Storage Changes

A change in the water level of any well (change in head) is a measure of a change in storage in the ground-water reservoir in the neighborhood of the open interval of the well. Thus, a rising water level in a well represents an increase in storage and a declining water level represents a decrease in storage in the ground-water reservoir. This situation is analogous to changes in water level in surface-water reservoirs. However, the relation between changes in water levels in wells and changes in the volume of water in storage is considerably more complex in ground-water reservoirs than in surface-water reservoirs (see Box A).

Even in aquifers and parts of aquifers that are not stressed by pumping wells, water levels in wells change continuously in response to changes in natural rates of recharge and discharge in the ground-water-flow system. Water levels in many wells exhibit an approximate annual cycle—water levels are highest during months of highest recharge, commonly the spring of the year, and lowest during months of lowest recharge, commonly the summer and early fall. In addition, large changes in recharge and discharge occur from year to year, which results in a potentially significant rise and decline in water levels during wet and dry years, respectively (Figure 17).

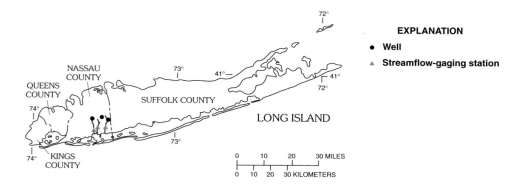

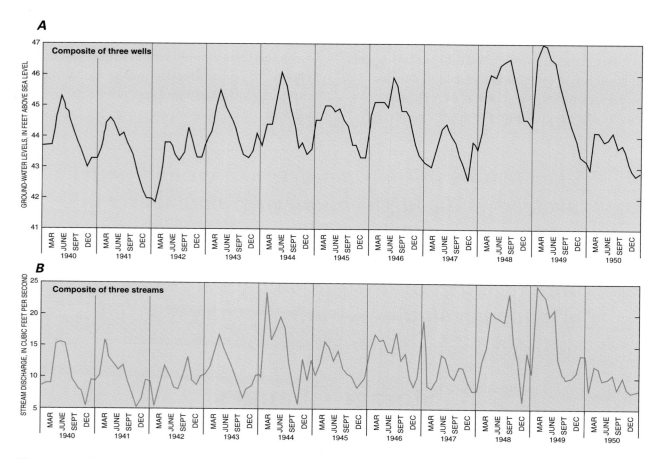

Figure 17. *Composite average monthly (A) ground-water levels in selected wells and (B) discharge of selected streams in Nassau County, Long Island, New York for the period 1940-50. (Modified from Franke and McClymonds, 1972.)*

The highly transmissive surficial deposits of sand and gravel, low relief, and humid climate of Long Island create ideal conditions for good hydraulic connection between the unconfined aquifer and numerous small streams. Before development more than 90 percent of total streamflow was derived from ground-water inflow; thus, these streams have been described as "ground-water drains." The good correspondence between ground-water levels in the unconfined aquifer and flow in nearby streams reflects the fact that in this ground-water system most of the streamflow is derived from ground water and there is good connection between the two systems.

46

Declines in heads and associated reductions in storage in response to pumping can be large compared to changes in unstressed ground-water systems. For example, declines in heads as a result of intense pumping can reach several hundred feet in some hydrogeologic settings. Widespread pumping that is sufficient to cause regional declines in heads can result in several unwanted effects. For example: (1) regional declines in heads may represent large decreases in aquifer storage, particularly in unconfined aquifers; (2) some wells may become dry because the lower heads are below the screened or open intervals of these wells; (3) pumping costs will increase because the vertical distance that ground water must be lifted to the land surface increases; (4) locally, the rate of movement of contaminated ground water and the likelihood that the contaminated ground water will be intercepted by a pumping well are increased; and (5) pumping of ground water may result in land subsidence or intrusion of saline ground water in some hydrogeologic settings. Because large and widespread changes in heads in aquifers are of interest to water managers and users of the ground-water resource, maps of heads (water levels) often are prepared periodically for individual, heavily pumped aquifers by water agencies. Comparisons of these synoptic-head maps permit changes in ground-water levels in wells to be documented through time for individual aquifers. Such histories of head change sometimes serve as the basis and catalyst for initiatives to manage the affected ground-water reservoir. The following examples illustrate aquifer response to pumping and associated changes in storage in different environmental settings.

High Plains aquifer—Let's first return to a previous example, the High Plains aquifer (see section on "Ground-Water Development, Sustainability, and Water Budgets"). Ground-water pumping from this unconfined aquifer has resulted in the largest decrease in storage of any major aquifer in the Nation. In parts of the central and southern High Plains, more than 50 percent of the predevelopment saturated thickness has been dewatered (see Figure 10B). The water table continues to decline under much of the High Plains. During the past two decades, however, monitoring of water levels in wells indicates an overall reduced rate of decline of the water table (McGuire and Sharpe, 1997). This change is attributed to improved irrigation and cultivation practices, decreases in irrigated acreage, and above normal precipitation during this period. In parts of the High Plains, water-level rises have occurred because of seepage losses from surface-water irrigation or the recovery of local cones of depression as a result of decreased pumpage.

High Plains Aquifer: Egg Carton or Bathtub

A key question related to ground-water sustainability in intensively irrigated areas is the extent to which individual irrigators have incentive to consider the effect of their current pumping decisions on their own future pumping costs. For example, if an irrigator could be sure that water not pumped today would be available for use later, he or she might change their pumping strategy to use the water more efficiently over time.

As an example, in the early 1980's questions were posed in economic forecasting for the High Plains aquifer as to whether the aquifer could be treated, from an individual irrigator's point of view, as an "egg carton" or a "bathtub"

(Beattie, 1981). The egg carton analogy assumes that users of ground water are not seriously subject to depletion by the actions of neighboring irrigators because of the local nature of the cone of depression formed around an individual pumped well, particularly for an unconfined aquifer (see Box A). The bathtub analogy, on the other hand, views the aquifer as a common pool in which water levels respond to pumping as though water were being withdrawn from a bathtub or lake. In such a system, an increase in withdrawal by one irrigator immediately translates into an increase in pumping lifts for all irrigators.

The actual situation lies somewhere between these two analogies. Water pumped by a well is withdrawn from the aquifer within the vicinity of the well; however, the cumulative effects of pumping many neighboring wells over many years result in regional water-level declines. These regional declines in water levels limit the influence that an individual irrigator has over his or her own future pumping lifts. The local effects of changes in the magnitude and direction of gradients in the water table also must be considered. That is, the net effects of the reduced pumping from a well will be distributed over an area that increases with time and that may not be limited to the well owner's property. The end result is that the decreases in water withdrawals do not result in an equivalent future increase in ground-water storage directly under the pumped area.

A hypothetical pumping scenario illustrates these effects (Alley and Schefter, 1987). In this scenario, pumping is reduced from a base level by 25 percent for 10 years within management areas of various sizes in the High Plains. The effect of the reduced pumping was simulated for 10 years and 20 years from the start of the water-conservation program; that is, at the end of 10 years of conservation and at 10 years after conservation ended. The results, shown in Figure D–1 for both time periods, demonstrate that individual irrigators operating at the local scale have limited ability to "bank" water to decrease their future pumping lifts, but that opportunity exists at larger management scales to effectively reduce future pumping lifts. For example, after 20 years much less than 10 percent of the conserved water remains under areas of a few square miles or less (the size of many farms); but this increases to about 60 percent for areas of 250 square miles and to more than 85 percent for management areas in excess of 1,000 square miles. The results illustrate the potential usefulness of ground-water management areas and provide some insight into the effectiveness of different size areas.

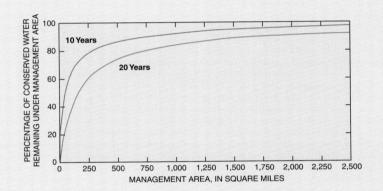

Figure D–1. *Percentage of water conserved by reduced pumping that provides increased ground-water storage under hypothetical management areas of different size overlying the High Plains aquifer. (Modified from Alley and Schefter, 1987.)*

49

Nassau County, New York—The response of an unconfined aquifer to stress in a humid climate that results from urban land-use practices is exemplified by the upper glacial aquifer on Long Island. It was noted previously that prior to installation of an extensive sewer system, a large proportion of the water pumped on Long Island for public supply and commercial use was returned to this unconfined aquifer by septic systems. After installation, water that formerly recharged the upper glacial aquifer from septic systems now was discharged directly into the ocean. This loss of

recharge represented a significant change to the water budget of the ground-water system and resulted in a loss in storage of water in the upper glacial aquifer.

The effects of installation of the sewer system on aquifer storage in Long Island are reflected in the water-level record shown in Figure 18 for a well completed in the upper glacial aquifer in west-central Nassau County, an area where an extensive sewer system began operation in the early 1950's. The upper horizontal line in Figure 18 (water level equals 68 feet above sea

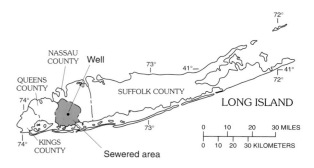

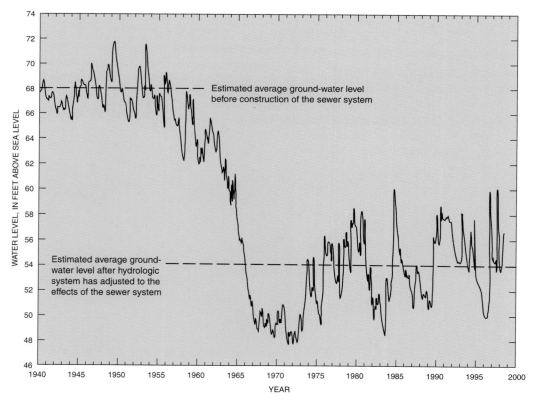

Figure 18. *Water-level record for a well completed in the upper glacial aquifer in west-central Nassau County, Long Island, New York.*

50

level) represents an average water-table altitude at the well before installation of the sewer system. The fluctuations in water level around the average value represent a response to the annual cycle of recharge and evapotranspiration and the differences in this cycle from year to year. The sewer system achieved close to its maximum discharge by the mid-1960's for the existing population in the sewered area. The lower horizontal line (water level equals 54 feet above sea level) represents the average water level after the hydrologic system had adjusted to the effects of installation of the sewer system. The water-level fluctuations around the lower horizontal line again reflect annual recharge and evapotranspiration cycles.

Installation of the sewer system has resulted in an areally extensive (several tens of square miles) loss of storage in the unconfined aquifer. The most obvious undesirable effect of the lowered water-table elevations has been marked decreases in the flow and length of small, ground-water-fed streams in the area. The positive effect of installing the sewer system has been to reduce recharge of contaminated water from septic systems and thereby help maintain the quality of shallow ground water and the deeper ground water that is hydraulically connected to the shallow ground water.

Chicago/Milwaukee area—The long history of ground-water withdrawals from the Cambrian-Ordovician aquifer in the Chicago and Milwaukee areas is a well-documented example of the effects of heavy pumpage on heads in a confined aquifer. The first documented deep well in the Chicago area was drilled in 1864 to a depth of 711 feet and flowed at the land surface at a rate of 400 gallons per minute. During the next decades and into the 20th century as the Chicago metropolitan area grew, the number of wells, the areal extent of pumping, and the total withdrawals from this aquifer increased substantially. Maximum withdrawals, about 180 million gallons per day, and maximum declines in heads of about 800 feet for the Cambrian-Ordovician aquifer, occurred in the eight-county Chicago area in about 1980

(Figure 19). Since 1980, many public water suppliers in the Chicago area have shifted their source of water from ground water to additional withdrawals from Lake Michigan. This shift has resulted in a significant decrease in total withdrawals from the aquifer and a general recovery (increase) of heads in the areas of decreased withdrawal (Figure 20). Pumping continues in all parts of the Chicago and Milwaukee area, however, and may be increasing in some parts, so that heads in some localities may still be decreasing.

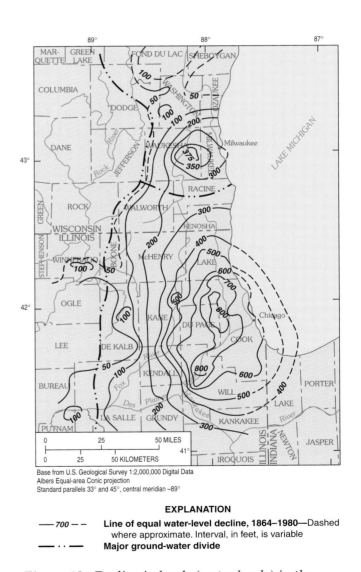

Base from U.S. Geological Survey 1:2,000,000 Digital Data
Albers Equal-area Conic projection
Standard parallels 33° and 45°, central meridian –89°

EXPLANATION

—— 700 – –   **Line of equal water-level decline, 1864–1980**—Dashed where approximate. Interval, in feet, is variable

—— ·· ——   **Major ground-water divide**

Figure 19. *Decline in heads (water levels) in the Cambrian-Ordovician confined aquifer, Chicago and Milwaukee areas, 1864-1980. (Modified from Avery, 1995.)*

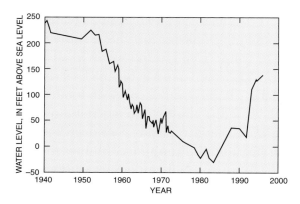

Figure 20. *Representative trend of water levels for a deep well in Cook County, Chicago area, since 1940. (From Visocky, 1997.)*

The volume of the cone of depression in the Chicago and Milwaukee area is large, even with the present decrease in withdrawal rates. A principal concern has been the possibility of beginning to dewater the confined aquifer and effectively convert it to an unconfined aquifer. This possibility was imminent at the center of the cone of depression in 1980 and was avoided by the subsequent decrease in withdrawal rates in this critical area.

The sustainability of confined aquifer systems like the Cambrian-Ordovician aquifer is typically controlled by the proximity of pumping centers to recharge and discharge areas or by the hydraulic connection with other aquifer systems. Walton (1964) defined the "practical sustained yield" of the Cambrian-Ordovician aquifer as

the maximum amount of water that can be continuously withdrawn from existing pumping centers without eventually dewatering the most productive water-yielding formation. Using this definition, Walton estimated the practical sustained yield to be about 46 million gallons per day. He noted that with the existing distribution of pumping centers, the practical sustained yield was limited not by the rate of replenishment in recharge areas but by the rate at which water can move eastward through the aquifer from recharge areas. Walton estimated that the practical sustained yield could be increased more than 40 percent to about 65 million gallons per day by (1) increasing the number of pumping centers, (2) shifting centers of pumping toward the recharge area, and (3) spacing wells at greater distances.

In all but the deeply buried parts of the Cambrian-Ordovician aquifer in the Chicago and Milwaukee area, the water is chemically suited for all uses. Thus, water quality has not been a major factor affecting the use of this aquifer. Because of their greater depth, however, confined aquifers often contain saline water or are hydraulically connected to other aquifers and confining units that contain water with high dissolved-solids concentration. Declines in head in the confined aquifer can cause the movement of poor quality water from surrounding aquifers (or confining units), which may limit development of the aquifer more than declines in heads and aquifer storage.

Kings County, New York—The history of ground-water development in Kings County (Brooklyn), Long Island, New York since the early 1900's is a well-documented example of a complete cycle of intensive development with significant decreases in heads and reduction in storage in the unconfined aquifer accompanied by intrusion of saline ground water, followed by a decrease in total pumpage and a gradual recovery of heads. In 1903, total ground-water withdrawals in Kings County were about 30 million gallons per day. Available information on the altitude of the water table indicates no obvious cones of depression at this time (Figure 21). Total pumpage in Kings County peaked in the 1920's to early 1940's (maximum annual pumpage about 75 million gallons per day). As shown in Figure 21, water levels in 1936 were near or below sea level throughout Kings County, and the cone of depression extended into southwestern Queens County.

In 1947, public-supply pumpage ceased in Kings County. The source of water for public supply changed to the upstate surface-water system that supplies New York City through water tunnels. Furthermore, legislation was implemented during this period that required "wastewater" (including air-conditioning water) from some industrial/commercial uses be recharged to the aquifer system through wells. Concurrently, and partly as a result of these changes, industrial pumpage declined to a long-term stable rate of slightly less than 10 million gallons per day. These changes are reflected in the water-table map of 1965 shown in Figure 21 in which heads have risen throughout Kings County and are at or below sea level only in northern parts of the county. Subsequent maps show a small but continuing recovery of the water table.

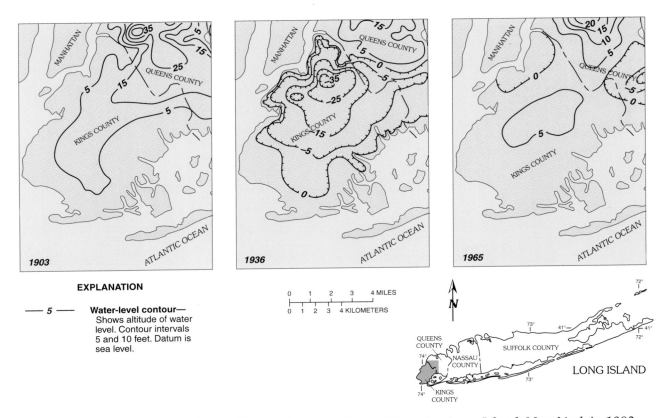

Figure 21. *Water-table altitudes in Kings and part of Queens Counties, Long Island, New York in 1903, 1936, and 1965. (Modified from Franke and McClymonds, 1972.)*

The history of ground-water development in Kings County has been influenced considerably by the strong hydraulic connection between the unconfined ground-water system and the surrounding bodies of saline surface water. The decision to stop pumping for public supply and to recharge high-quality wastewater back to the aquifer system was driven in large measure by concerns about ongoing and continuing intrusion of saline ground water into the naturally fresh part of the aquifer system. On the other hand, an unforeseen and undesirable effect of decreased pumpage and the accompanying rise in the altitude of the water table in Kings County is that basements of major buildings constructed in the 1920's and 1930's now lie below the water table and require continuous pumping of dewatering systems to keep them dry.

Commonalities in the preceding four examples are noteworthy and include (1) the changes in storage resulted in observable changes in the ground-water system; (2) the changes in the ground-water system generally were viewed by local stakeholders as undesirable, at least to some extent; and (3) in at least three of the four examples, some response to mitigate the perceived undesirable effects of the change in storage was initiated. In examples such as the southern High Plains aquifer in Texas and New Mexico, and the unconfined aquifer in Brooklyn, New York, the long-term sustainability of the ground-water resource was perceived to be in jeopardy.

Subsidence

Land subsidence, which is a decline in land-surface elevation caused by removal of subsurface support, can result from a variety of human activities (Galloway and others, in press). Subsidence can severely damage structures such as wells, buildings, and highways, and creates problems in the design and operation of facilities for drainage, flood protection, and water conveyance. Human activities related to ground water cause land subsidence by three basic mechanisms: compaction of aquifer systems, dissolution and collapse of rocks that are relatively soluble in water (for example, limestone, dolomite, and evaporites such as salt and gypsum), and dewatering of organic soils.

Compaction of aquifer systems as a result of ground-water withdrawals and accompanying land subsidence is most common in heavily pumped alluvial aquifer systems that include clay and silt layers. As heads in the aquifer system decline due to pumping, some of the support for the overlying material previously provided by the pressurized water filling the sediment pore space shifts to the granular skeleton of the aquifer system, increasing the intergranular pressure (load). Because sand and gravel deposits are relatively incompressible, the increased intergranular load has a negligible effect on these aquifer materials. However, clay and silt layers comprising confining units and interbeds can be very compressible as water is squeezed from these layers in response to the hydraulic gradient caused by pumping.

So long as the intergranular load remains less than any previous maximum load, the deformation of the aquifer system is reversible. However, when long-term declines in head increase the intergranular load beyond the previous maximum load, the structure of clay and silt layers may undergo significant rearrangement, resulting in irreversible aquifer system compaction and land subsidence. The amount of compaction is a function of the thickness and vertical hydraulic conductivity of the clay and silt layers, and the type and structure of the clays and silts. Because of the low hydraulic conductivity of clay and silt layers, the compaction of these layers can continue for months or years after water levels stabilize in the aquifer. In confined aquifer systems that contain significant clay and silt layers and are subject to large-scale ground-water withdrawals, the volume of water derived from irreversible compaction commonly can range from 10 to 30 percent of the total volume of water pumped (Galloway and others, in press). This represents a one-time mining of stored ground water and a permanent reduction in the storage capacity of the aquifer system.

The first recognized land subsidence in the United States from aquifer compaction as a response to ground-water withdrawals was in the area now known as "Silicon Valley" in California. Other areas experiencing significant land subsidence from ground-water withdrawals include the San Joaquin Valley of California (see Box B), the alluvial basins of south-central Arizona (Figure 22), Las Vegas Valley in Nevada, the Houston-Galveston area of Texas, and the Lancaster area near Los Angeles, California.

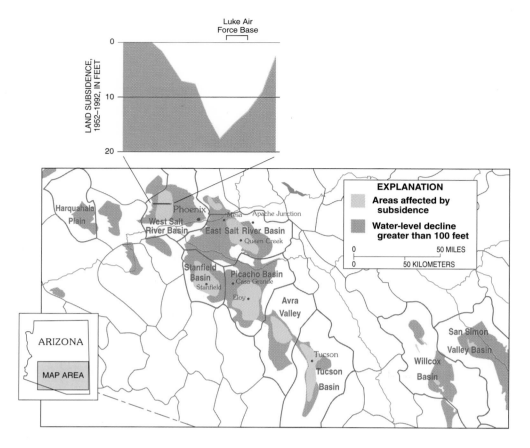

Figure 22. *Land subsidence in south-central Arizona. (Modified from Carpenter, in press.)*

Ground-water development for agriculture in the basin-fill aquifers of south-central Arizona began in the late 1800's, and by the 1940's many of the basins had undergone intensive ground-water development. Ground-water depletion has been widespread over these basins, and locally, water-level declines have exceeded 300 feet. These water-level declines have resulted in regional subsidence, exceeding 10 feet in some areas. A profile near Luke Air Force Base illustrates that subsidence is greater near the center of basins, where the aggregate thickness of the fine-grained sediments is generally greater. In conjunction with widespread subsidence, numerous earth fissures have formed at and near the margins of subsiding basins or near exposed or shallow buried bedrock.

In many areas of the arid Southwest, earth fissures are associated with land subsidence. Earth fissures are caused by horizontal movement of sediment that occurs during compaction. These features start out as narrow cracks, an inch or less in width. They intercept surface drainage and can erode to widths of tens of feet at the surface and may extend more than 100 feet below the land surface. Fissures may be a few hundred feet to miles in length. One extraordinary fissure in the Picacho Basin, northwest of Tucson, Arizona, is 10 miles long.

Sign warning motorists of subsidence hazard was erected after an earth fissure damaged a road in Pima County, Arizona (left photograph). Earth fissure near Picacho, Arizona (right photograph). (Photographs by S.R. Anderson, U.S. Geological Survey.)

Subsidence also occurs from local sinkhole collapse in areas underlain by limestone, dolomite, and other soluble rocks. Areas susceptible to sinkhole collapse are particularly common in the humid Eastern United States. Sinkhole development occurs naturally but may be enhanced by human activities, such as diversion and impoundment of surface water and pumping of ground water. Ground-water pumping can induce sinkholes by reducing the buoyant support of cavity walls and ceilings or by reducing the cohesion of loose, unconsolidated materials overlying preexisting sinkholes. The effects of ground-water pumping on sinkhole development can result from long-term declines in water levels or in response to rapid fluctuations of water levels caused by pumping wells. Some notable examples of rapid sinkhole development have occurred in the Southeastern United States. Though the collapse features tend to be highly localized, their effects can extend well beyond the collapse zone as a result of the introduction of contaminants from the land surface to the ground-water systems.

Finally, land subsidence can occur when organic soils are drained for agriculture or other purposes. Causes include compaction, desiccation, wind erosion, and oxidation of drained organic soil layers. These effects commonly are associated with the purposeful draining of the land surface but also may occur as a result of ground-water pumping near wetlands and other poorly drained areas. Subsidence at rates of an inch or more per year as a result of drainage has been observed over large areas such as the Sacramento-San Joaquin Delta in California and the Florida Everglades (Galloway and others, in press).

Development of a new irrigation well in west-central Florida triggered hundreds of sinkholes over a 20-acre area. The sinkholes ranged in size from less than 1 foot to more than 150 feet in diameter. (Photograph by Ann B. Tihansky, U.S. Geological Survey; see person in center for scale.)

WATER-QUALITY FACTORS AFFECTING GROUND-WATER SUSTAINABILITY

Previous chapters have discussed quantities of water recharging, flowing through, and discharging from the ground-water system and quantities of water stored in the system. This brief discussion of ground-water quality adds a further dimension to ground-water resource sustainability; namely, the question of the suitability of ground water for different uses. Various measures of water quality such as taste and odor, microbial content, and dissolved concentrations of naturally occurring and manufactured chemical constituents define the suitability of water for different uses.

The availability of ground water and the suitability of its quality for different uses are inextricably intertwined. To take an extreme example, salt brines having very high dissolved-solids concentrations occur adjacent to fresh ground water almost everywhere. Although brines represent huge volumes of ground water in storage, these brines are not included in most inventories of available ground water because of their inherent unsuitability for almost all uses. Ground waters having somewhat lower dissolved-solids concentrations may be suitable for some uses but not for others. For example, some cattle can tolerate a higher dissolved-solids concentration in their drinking water than humans.

A key consideration in managing a ground-water resource is its vulnerability to sources of contamination that are located primarily at and near the land surface. Because of generally low ground-water velocities, once contaminants have reached the water table, their movement to nearby surface-water discharge areas or to deeper parts of the ground-water-flow system is slow. For the same reason, once parts of an aquifer are contaminated, the time required for a return to better water-quality conditions as a result of natural processes is long, even after the original sources of contamination are no longer active. Ground-water-quality remediation projects generally are very expensive and commonly are only partly successful. In some settings, steep gradients caused by ground-water pumping can greatly increase the rate at which contaminants move to deeper ground water. For these reasons, State and Federal environmental

The availability of ground water and the suitability of its quality for different uses are inextricably intertwined.

agencies seek to protect the ground-water resource by stressing regulatory efforts to prevent ground-water contamination.

Contamination of ground water is not always a result of the introduction of contaminants by human activities. Possible natural contaminants include trace elements such as arsenic and selenium, radionuclides such as radon, and high concentrations of commonly occurring dissolved constituents.

The first two subsections below involve two of the most significant linkages in hydrology—the land-surface/water-table connection and the ground-water/surface-water connection. The third subsection, saltwater intrusion, involves movement of naturally occurring, highly saline ground water into parts of adjacent aquifers that contain less saline water. Pumping of the less saline (commonly potable) ground water generally causes this movement.

Land-Surface /Water-Table Connection

In principle, virtually any human activity at and near the land surface can be a source of contaminants to ground water as long as water and possibly other fluids move from the land surface to the water table. Sources of chemicals introduced to ground water in this way include fertilizers, manure, and pesticides applied to agricultural lands; landfills; industrial-discharge lagoons; leaking gasoline storage tanks; cesspools and septic tanks; and domestically used chemicals. These sources commonly are classified as "point" or "nonpoint" sources. For example, industrial lagoons, leaking storage tanks, and landfills are considered to be point sources. A considerable number of these sources and associated contaminant plumes have undergone intensive studies followed by a remediation program. Many of the chemicals associated with point sources—for example, gasoline and other manufactured organic chemicals—even at very low concentrations,

render the contaminated ground water highly undesirable or useless as a source of domestic or public supply.

Croplands are a primary nonpoint source of contamination because of their large areal extent and significant applications per unit area of possible contaminants (fertilizers and pesticides) to ground water. Irrigated agriculture also has noteworthy effects on ground-water (and surface-water) quality. Increased areal recharge from excess irrigation-water applications results in the potential for increased transport of contaminants from the land surface to ground water. Also, a marked increase in dissolved-solids concentrations in soil water and shallow ground water may result from evaporation of irrigation water during delivery of the water to the crops and from transpiration of the applied water by the crops. In addition to cropland, agricultural activities include numerous point sources such as animal feedlots, waste lagoons, and storage sheds for agricultural chemicals.

Although the area occupied by urban land is small compared to the total area of the Nation, the diverse activities in urban areas provide innumerable point sources of contamination that can affect the quality of shallow ground water. From a regional perspective, urban land can be considered as a nonpoint source that exhibits a wide range in water quality. These effects on ground-water quality are particularly important from a water-management viewpoint if the water-table aquifer beneath urban land is used or could be used as a source of water supply.

A noteworthy effort to protect ground-water quality and the sustainability of the local ground-water resource, specifically to protect the quality of ground water that is pumped from public-supply wells, is the wellhead protection programs undertaken by the U.S. Environmental Protection Agency and the States. The approach of these programs is to estimate areas at the water table that contribute recharge to public-supply wells (Figure 23) and then to implement ground-water protection practices on the overlying land surface. Because many uncertainties exist in estimating areas contributing recharge to pumping wells (particularly for well-screen placements at some distance below the water table), and because areas contributing recharge may be located a considerable distance from the pumped wells, implementing ground-water protection practices at the land surface often poses considerable challenges.

Figure 23. Area contributing recharge to a single discharging well in a simplified hypothetical ground-water system: (A) cross-sectional view, and (B) map view. (Modified from Reilly and Pollock, 1993.)

The area contributing recharge to a pumping well can be defined as the surface area at the water table where water entering the ground-water system eventually flows to the well. If the system is at equilibrium, this area must provide an amount of recharge that balances the amount of water being discharged from the well. Thus, lower areal recharge rates result in larger contributing areas of wells. If a nearby surface-water body also contributes water to the discharging well, the area contributing recharge is reduced and is a function not only of the areal recharge rate but also of the amount of water obtained from the surface-water body. Depending on factors that describe the three-dimensional flow system and the placement of the well, the area contributing recharge to a well does not necessarily have to include the location of the well itself.

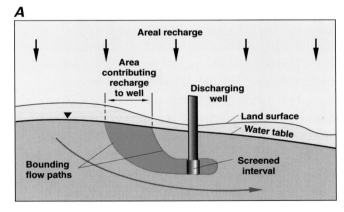

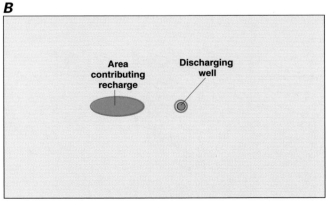

Ground-Water/Surface-Water Connection

The movement of water in both directions between ground-water systems and surface-water bodies has been discussed previously in this report. Chemical constituents are transported along with the moving water. Thus, contaminants in surface water can be transported into adjacent ground-water systems, and contaminants in ground water can be transported into adjacent surface-water bodies.

Because ground water commonly is a major component of streamflow, the quality of discharging ground water potentially can affect the quality of the receiving stream in many hydrologic settings (Figure 24). Because the proportion of streamflow contributed by ground water can vary greatly throughout the year, seasonal variations in the effects of ground-water quality on stream-water quality can occur.

Reductions in the quantity of ground water discharged to a stream as a result of pumping may have significant consequences where this discharge significantly dilutes the concentration of contaminants introduced to streams from point sources and surface runoff. In such situations, streamflow capture by pumping wells may reduce the contaminant-dilution capacity of the stream during periods of low flow below the dilution capacity assumed in setting discharge permits for the stream.

Contributing areas to wells often include surface-water bodies, and increasing attention is being placed on surface water as a potential source of contamination to wells. Possible contamination by induced infiltration of surface water adds several dimensions to the protection of ground water. These include consideration of the upstream drainage basin as part of the "contributing area" to the well and greater consideration of microbial contamination. Contaminated surface water may have a significant effect on the sustainable development of ground water near streams or on the need for treatment of ground water prior to use. Among the settings of greatest concern for contamination of ground water by streams are karst terrains where aquifers are hydraulically connected by sinkholes or other conduits that can channel river water directly into an aquifer with little or no filtration (see Box E).

In many aquifers, large changes in chemical oxidation conditions, organic-matter content, and microbial activity occur within a relatively thin (a few feet or even inches) zone or interface between ground water and surface water. Thus, conditions near the interface between ground water and surface water can significantly affect the transport and fate of nutrients, metals, organic compounds, and other contaminants between the two resources. Reactions at this interface commonly decrease the concentrations that might be transported between surface water and ground water (Winter and others, 1998).

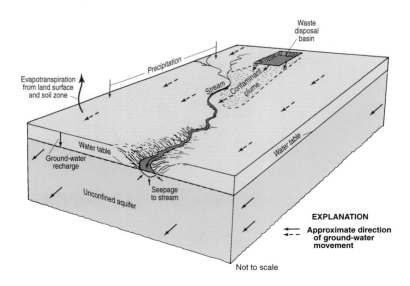

Figure 24. *Simplified representation of a contaminant plume in ground water.*

In this hypothetical example, sufficient time has elapsed for part of the plume of contaminated ground water to reach and discharge into a nearby stream. As shown, the stream intercepts the plume as it reaches the stream. In some situations, depending upon the geometry of the ground-water-flow system and the location of the plume in the flow system, part or all of the plume may flow under the stream and contaminate ground water on the other side of the stream.

The Connection Between Surface-Water Quality and Ground-Water Quality in a Karst Aquifer

The Upper Floridan aquifer, which is the sole source of water supply for Valdosta, Georgia, and much of the surrounding area, receives large volumes of direct discharge from the Withlacoochee River through sinkholes in the streambed or off-channel. A highly interconnected conduit system has developed in the Upper Floridan aquifer in this area, which extends at least 15 miles from the sinkhole area. Chloride and isotopic data were used by Plummer and others (1998) to map the percentage of Withlacoochee River water in ground water in the Upper Floridan aquifer (Figure E–1). These data indicate that ground water in parts of the Upper Floridan aquifer contains high percentages of recently recharged Withlacoochee River water. Plummer and others (1998) note that, although the patterns shown in Figure E–1 are generally true over the area, extreme variations can occur at a given location, as would be expected because of the large variations and discontinuities in hydraulic properties in the karst environment and time-varying inflows of river water into the aquifer.

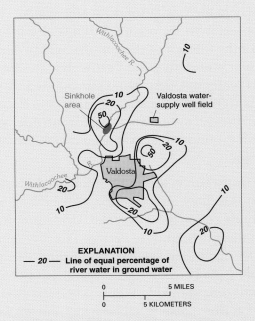

EXPLANATION
— 20 — Line of equal percentage of river water in ground water

0   5 MILES

0   5 KILOMETERS

Figure E–1. *Estimated percentage of Withlacoochee River water in ground water in the Upper Floridan aquifer, June 1991. (Modified from Plummer and others, 1998.)*

Sinkhole near the Withlacoochee River. (Photograph by Richard E. Krause, U.S. Geological Survey.)

The strong connection between the Withlacoochee River and ground water in the Valdosta area has created concerns about the potential for contamination of ground-water supplies by contaminants in the river. There also are concerns about the effects of natural organic matter in the river water. For example, in the early 1980's, it was recognized that chlorination of aquifer water produced disinfection by-products in excess of drinking-water standards. This occurred as a result of reaction of chlorine with the high amounts of natural organic matter in the river water recharged to the aquifer.

The original wells for Valdosta were near the city, in the areas where the aquifer contains a high percentage of river water. The city completed a new set of water-supply wells in the well field indicated in Figure E–1, in an area where the aquifer contains a relatively low percentage of river water. Even with this added level of assurance, it is still necessary to protect the surface waters that supply the aquifer. The source area of concern for ground water is the entire Withlacoochee River Basin upstream from Valdosta.

Saltwater Intrusion

The fresh ground-water resource of the United States is surrounded laterally and below by saline water. This is most evident along coastal areas where the fresh ground-water system comes into contact with the oceans, but it is also true in much of the interior of the country where deep saline water underlies the freshwater. The fresh ground-water resource being surrounded by salt-water is significant because, under some circumstances, the saltwater can move (or intrude) into the fresh ground-water system, making the water unpotable.

Freshwater is less dense than saline water and tends to flow on top of the surrounding or underlying saline ground water. Under natural conditions, the boundary between freshwater and saltwater maintains a stable equilibrium, as shown in Figure 25A. The boundary typically is not sharp and distinct as shown in Figure 25A, but rather is a gradation from fresh to saline water known as the zone of diffusion, zone of dispersion, or the transition zone. When water is pumped from an aquifer that contains or is near saline ground water, the saltwater/freshwater boundary will move in response to this pumping. That is, any pumpage will cause some movement in the boundary between the freshwater and the surrounding saltwater. If the boundary moves far enough,

some wells become saline, thus contaminating the water supply. The location and magnitude of the ground-water withdrawals with respect to the location of the saltwater determines how quickly and by how much the saltwater moves. Even if the lateral regional movement of saltwater is negligible, individual wells located near the saltwater/freshwater boundary can become saline as a result of significant local drawdowns that cause underlying saltwater to "upcone" into the well (Figure 25B).

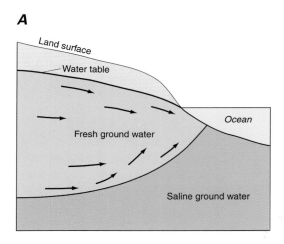

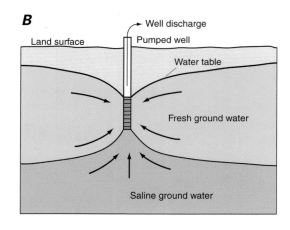

Figure 25. *Relation of fresh and saline ground water. (Modified from U.S. Geological Survey, 1984.)*

(A) In coastal areas, fresh ground water discharges to the surrounding saline surface-water bodies by flowing over the denser saline ground water. (B) In both coastal and inland areas, large drawdowns in an individual well can cause underlying saline water to migrate upward into the well and cause contamination of the water being discharged.

In 1969, the Task Committee on Saltwater Intrusion of the American Society of Civil Engineers (1969) indicated that saltwater intrusion of some type is an existing problem in nearly every State. Examples of saltwater intrusion are especially numerous along the coasts (U.S. Geological Survey, 1984). Some prominent examples follow.

Los Angeles and Orange Counties in California operate artificial-recharge programs to control saltwater intrusion caused by ground-water withdrawals. In Hawaii, several aquifers susceptible to saltwater intrusion underlie the island of Oahu. In Florida, saltwater intrusion occurs in the Jacksonville, Tampa, and Miami areas. Farther north on the Atlantic Coast, saltwater intrusion is occurring near Brunswick and Savannah, Georgia, and on Hilton Head Island, South Carolina. In New Jersey, aquifers underlying parts of Atlantic, Gloucester, Monmouth, Cape May, Ocean, and Salem Counties are being affected by saltwater intrusion. The threat of saltwater intrusion is always present on Long Island, New York, and Cape Cod, Massachusetts, because saltwater bodies surround both localities. A specific example of saltwater intrusion into the Old Bridge aquifer of New Jersey (Schaefer and Walker, 1981) is shown in Figure 26.

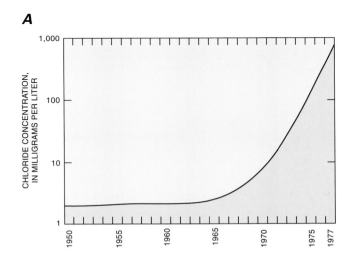

Figure 26. *Saltwater intrusion into the Old Bridge aquifer, New Jersey. (Modified from Schaefer and Walker, 1981.)*

(A) A composite graph of chloride concentration in water samples from wells screened at about the same depth in the Union Beach Borough well field. Chloride concentration in water samples from the Union Beach well field increased significantly above background levels beginning in about 1970 and increased steadily after that time. (B) As pumping in the area caused water levels to decline below sea level, saline ground water moved landward and caused the increase in chloride (and dissolved solids) in wells near the shore. Because of the increasing chloride and dissolved solids, pumpage was curtailed in the 1980's, and the well field was abandoned in the early 1990's and replaced by wells farther inland.

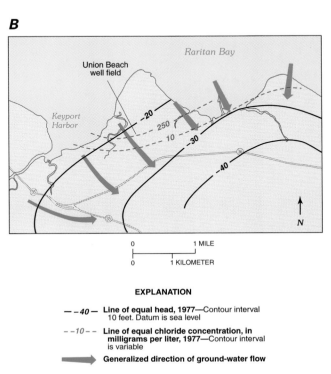

EXPLANATION

— –40 — **Line of equal head, 1977**—Contour interval 10 feet. Datum is sea level

– –10 – – **Line of equal chloride concentration, in milligrams per liter, 1977**—Contour interval is variable

Generalized direction of ground-water flow

An inland area where saltwater intrusion is an important issue is the Mississippi River alluvial plain in Arkansas. For example, ground-water withdrawals from the alluvial aquifer for irrigation near Brinkley, Arkansas, have caused upward movement of saline water from the underlying Sparta aquifer into the alluvial aquifer (Morris and Bush, 1986). A confining unit separating the aquifers is discontinuous, and the intrusion appears to occur mainly where the confining unit is absent.

Many of the deeper aquifers in the central part of the United States contain saline water.

Withdrawals from the overlying aquifers in these areas increase the potential for saltwater intrusion from below.

In summary, the intrusion of saltwater or mixing of fresh ground water with the surrounding saltwater, caused by withdrawals of freshwater from the ground-water system, can make the resource unsuitable for use. Thus, ground-water development plans should take into account potential changes in water quality that might occur because of saltwater intrusion.

MEETING THE CHALLENGES OF GROUND-WATER SUSTAINABILITY

As we have seen, the sustainability of ground-water resources is a function of many factors, including decreases in ground-water storage, reductions in streamflow and lake levels, loss of wetland and riparian ecosystems, land subsidence, saltwater intrusion, and changes in ground-water quality. Each ground-water system and development situation is unique and requires an analysis adjusted to the nature of the water issues faced, including the social, economic, and legal constraints that must be taken into account. A key challenge for achieving ground-water sustainability is to frame the hydrologic implications of various alternative management strategies in such a way that they can be properly evaluated.

Ground-water scientists have developed an expanding capability to address issues associated with the development and sustainability of ground-water resources. Early efforts focused on methods of evaluating the effects of ground-water pumping on an aquifer's long-term capacity to yield water to wells. Subsequently, methods were applied to evaluate various effects of ground-water development on surface-water bodies, land subsidence, and saltwater intrusion. Starting in the late 1970's, increasing concerns about contamination of ground water by human activities led to an awareness of the great difficulty and expense of cleaning up contaminated aquifers and drew attention to the importance of prevention of ground-water contamination. With time, it has become clear that the chemical, biological, and physical aspects of ground-water systems are interrelated and require an integrated analysis, and that many issues involving the quantity, quality, and ecological aspects of surface water are interrelated with ground water. Thus, ground-water hydrologists are challenged continually by the need to provide greater refinement to their analyses and to address new problems and issues as they arise.

A key challenge for achieving ground-water sustainability is to frame the hydrologic implications of various alternative management strategies in such a way that they can be properly evaluated.

67

The Importance of Ground-Water Data

The foundation of any good ground-water analysis, including those analyses whose objective is to propose and evaluate alternative management strategies, is the availability of high-quality data. Principal types of data commonly required are listed in Table 2. Some, such as precipitation data, are generally available and relatively easy to obtain at the time of a hydrologic analysis. Other data and information, such as geologic and hydrogeologic maps, can require years to develop. Still other data, such as a history of water levels in different parts of ground-water systems, require foresight in order to obtain measurements over time, if they are to be available at all. Thus, a key starting point for assuring a sustainable future for any ground-water system is development of a comprehensive hydrogeologic data base over time. As examples, these data would include depths and thicknesses of hydrogeologic units from lithologic and geophysical well logs, water-level measurements to allow construction of predevelopment water-level maps for major aquifers as well as water-level maps at various times during development, ground-water sampling to document pre- and post-development water quality, and simultaneous measurements of streamflow and stream quality during low flows to indicate possible contributions of discharging ground water to surface-water quality. Many of the types of data and data compilations listed in Table 2 need to be viewed on maps. Thus, Geographic Information Systems (GIS) typically are an integral part of the data-base system to assist in organizing, storing, and displaying the substantial array of needed information.

The foundation of any good ground-water analysis, including those analyses whose objective is to propose and evaluate alternative management strategies, is the availability of high-quality data.

Table 2.—*Principal types of data and data compilations required for analysis of ground-water systems*

Physical Framework

Topographic maps showing the stream drainage network, surface-water bodies, landforms, cultural features, and locations of structures and activities related to water

Geologic maps of surficial deposits and bedrock

Hydrogeologic maps showing extent and boundaries of aquifers and confining units

Maps of tops and bottoms of aquifers and confining units

Saturated-thickness maps of unconfined (water-table) and confined aquifers

Average hydraulic conductivity maps for aquifers and confining units and transmissivity maps for aquifers

Maps showing variations in storage coefficient for aquifers

Estimates of age of ground water at selected locations in aquifers

Hydrologic Budgets and Stresses

Precipitation data

Evaporation data

Streamflow data, including measurements of gain and loss of streamflow between gaging stations

Maps of the stream drainage network showing extent of normally perennial flow, normally dry channels, and normally seasonal flow

Estimates of total ground-water discharge to streams

Measurements of spring discharge

Measurements of surface-water diversions and return flows

Quantities and locations of interbasin diversions

History and spatial distribution of pumping rates in aquifers

Amount of ground water consumed for each type of use and spatial distribution of return flows

Well hydrographs and historical head (water-level) maps for aquifers

Location of recharge areas (areal recharge from precipitation, losing streams, irrigated areas, recharge basins, and recharge wells), and estimates of recharge

Chemical Framework

Geochemical characteristics of earth materials and naturally occurring ground water in aquifers and confining units

Spatial distribution of water quality in aquifers, both areally and with depth

Temporal changes in water quality, particularly for contaminated or potentially vulnerable unconfined aquifers

Sources and types of potential contaminants

Chemical characteristics of artificially introduced waters or waste liquids

Maps of land cover/land use at different scales, depending on study needs

Streamflow quality (water-quality sampling in space and time), particularly during periods of low flow

---

Use of Ground-Water Computer Models

During the past several decades, computer simulation models for analyzing flow and solute transport in ground-water and surface-water systems have played an increasing role in the evaluation of alternative approaches to ground-water development and management. The use of these models has somewhat paralleled advances in computing systems. Ground-water models are an attempt to represent the essential features of the actual ground-water system by means of a mathematical counterpart. The underlying philosophy is that an understanding of the basic laws of physics, chemistry, and biology that describe ground-water flow and transport and an accurate description of the specific system under study will enable a quantitative representation of the cause and effect relationships for that system. Quantitative understanding of cause and effect relationships enables forecasts to be made for any defined set of conditions. However, such forecasts, which usually are outside the range of observed conditions, typically are limited by uncertainties due to sparse and inaccurate data, poor definition of stresses acting on the system, and errors in system conceptualization (Konikow and Bredehoeft, 1992). Although forecasts of future events that are based on model simulations are imprecise, they nevertheless may represent the best available decision-making information at a given time. Because of the usefulness of computer simulation for decision making, the basic construction of computer simulation models, as well as model forecasts, need to be updated periodically as the actual ground-water system continues to respond to the physical and chemical stresses imposed upon it and as new information on the ground-water system becomes available.

Although forecasts of future events that are based on model simulations are imprecise, they nevertheless may represent the best available decision-making information at a given time.

Refinement of Ground-Water System Understanding Through Time: Lessons from Post Audits

Computer simulation models of flow and transport are a principal means for evaluating the response of aquifer systems to ground-water withdrawals and other human activities. There is a tendency to view development of such models as a one-time activity. However, if a model is used to address questions about the future responses of a ground-water system that are of continuing significance to society, then field monitoring of the ground-water system should continue and the model should be reevaluated periodically to incorporate new information or new insights (Konikow and Reilly, 1999). For example, it might be desirable to add new capabilities to an existing model, such as interactions between ground water and surface-water bodies.

Ground-water models commonly are used to make forecasts for a decade or more in the future. Confidence in the reliability of a ground-water model is dependent in large part upon the quality and extent of historical data used to calibrate and test the model. In recent years, studies have been made of the accuracy of selected model forecasts several years after the date for which the forecasts had been made. Such studies, commonly referred to as post audits, offer a means to evaluate overall performance of a model and the nature and magnitude of model forecasting errors. Post audits also provide insights into possible future model enhancements.

As an example, a post audit was made for a ground-water model of the Blue River Basin, a heavily irrigated area in southeastern Nebraska. Forecasts of water-level declines for 1982 made by the model in 1965 were compared to measured 1982 water-level declines as shown in Figure F–1 (Alley and Emery, 1986). Overall, the forecasted and measured water-level declines were somewhat similar in magnitude, although clearly more complexity is shown by the measured water-level declines. Further examination during the post audit revealed that irrigation demand had been greatly underestimated for the forecast period between 1965 and 1982. If the actual ground-water withdrawals had been incorporated in the 1965 model, forecasted water-level drawdowns for 1982 would have been much greater than the measured drawdowns in 1982. Apparently, the aquifer storage coefficient used in the 1965 model was too low, and the model underestimated contributions to pumpage from sources other than depletion of aquifer storage. For example, streamflow depletion appears to have been underestimated.

One of the limitations of the Blue River Basin model was that ground-water development was relatively limited at the time of original model calibration. For example, the only area of significant water-level decline in 1965 was in the northern part of the basin. A common finding of post audits of ground-water model forecasts is that the time period for matching historical conditions in the original model was too short to capture important elements of the ground-water system in the model. Processes or boundary conditions that are insignificant under the initial, lower stress regime may become important under a different and generally larger set of imposed stresses. Thus, a conceptual model founded on observed behavior of a ground-water system may provide inaccurate forecasts if existing stresses are increased or new stresses are added. In addition, as illustrated by the Blue River Basin modeling study, future projections of water withdrawals typically are highly uncertain and need to be refined with time. The possibility of periodic refinement and reuse of ground-water models highlights the importance of thorough documentation and careful archiving of these models and continued monitoring of the ground-water system.

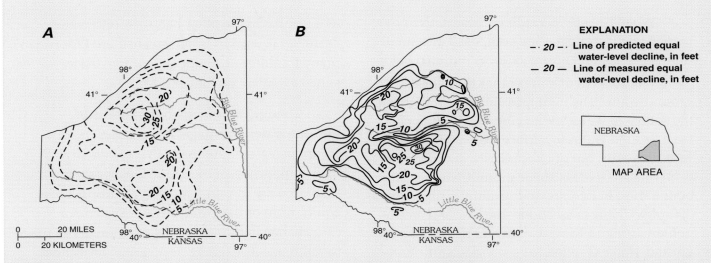

Figure F–1. (A) Predicted and (B) measured ground-water-level declines in the Blue River Basin from predevelopment to 1982. (Emery, 1965; Johnson and Pederson, 1983.)

Computer simulation models have value beyond their use as purely predictive tools. They commonly are used as learning tools to identify additional data that are required to better define and understand ground-water systems. Furthermore, computer simulation models have the capability to test and quantify the consequences of various errors and uncertainties in the information necessary to determine cause and effect relationships and related model-based forecasts. This capability, particularly as it relates to forecasts, may be the most important aspect of computer models in that information about the uncertainty of model forecasts can be defined, which in turn enables water managers to evaluate the significance, and possibly unexpected consequences, of their decisions.

If a model is used to address questions about the future responses of a ground-water system that are of continuing significance to society, then field monitoring of the ground-water system should continue and the model should be reevaluated periodically to incorporate new information or new insights.

Strategies for Sustainability

When broadly considered, alternative management strategies are composed of a small number of general approaches, as outlined below.

Use sources of water other than local ground water. The main possibilities are (1) shift the source of water, either completely or in part, from ground water to surface water, or (2) import water (usually, but not necessarily, surface water) from outside river-basin or ground-water system boundaries. In two previous examples given in the "Storage Changes" section—the Chicago metropolitan area and Kings County, Long Island—the ground-water systems were stressed sufficiently to cause undesirable effects, and surface-water sources were substituted for ground-water sources as a result. On the other hand, ground water currently is used or is being considered for use in many localities as a supplement for surface-water sources that are no longer adequate.

Change rates or spatial patterns of ground-water pumpage. Possibilities include (1) an increase in pumpage that results in a new equilibrium of the ground-water system, (2) a decrease in pumpage that results in a new equilibrium of the ground-water system, or (3) a change in the spatial distribution of pumpage to minimize its existing or potential unwanted effects. Management strategies might include varying combinations of these approaches.

Increase recharge to the ground-water system. Usual options include (1) pumpage designed to induce inflow from surface-water bodies, or (2) recharge of surface water or reused water (ground water or surface water) of good quality by surface spreading or injection through wells. Examples of several of these options are presented in Box G.

Decrease discharge from the ground-water system. Possibilities include pumpage that is designed to decrease discharge (1) to streams, lakes, or springs, or (2) from ground-water evapotranspiration. Both of these possibilities can have undesirable effects on surface-water bodies or on existing biological resources.

Change the volume of ground water in storage at different time scales. Possibilities include (1) managed short-term (time scale of months and years) increases and decreases in storage in the ground-water reservoir, which suggests that the ground-water reservoir might be managed at a time scale that is comparable to the management of surface-water reservoirs, or

(2) a continuing long-term (possible time scales of decades and centuries) decrease in ground-water storage. Of course, complete or almost complete depletion of aquifer storage is *not* a strategy for sustainability, but an extreme approach that may be considered in some situations.

Consideration of these general approaches indicates that they are not mutually exclusive; that is, the various approaches overlap, or the implementation of one approach will inevitably involve or cause the implementation of another. For example, changing rates or patterns of ground-water pumpage will lead to changes in the spatial patterns of recharge to or discharge from ground-water systems.

The short list of general approaches may suggest that proposing and evaluating alternative management strategies is deceptively simple. On the contrary, ground water is withdrawn from complex, three-dimensional systems, and many possible combinations of these approaches typically should be considered in developing management strategies for a particular ground-water system.

Innovative approaches that have been undertaken to enhance the sustainability of ground-water resources typically involve some combination of use of aquifers as storage reservoirs, conjunctive use of surface water and ground water, artificial recharge of water through wells or surface spreading, and the use of recycled or reclaimed water.

Examples of Innovative Approaches that Contribute to Ground-Water Sustainability

A variety of innovative approaches have been undertaken to enhance the sustainability of ground-water resources. These approaches typically involve some combination of the use of aquifers as storage reservoirs, conjunctive use of surface water and ground water, artificial recharge of water through wells or surface spreading, and use of recycled or reclaimed water. These approaches commonly lead to scientific questions about the extent and nature of ground-water and surface-water interactions, geochemical effects of mixing water from different sources with aquifer water, production and degradation of by-products from injection of treated water, and other issues.

Selected examples of innovative approaches that have been implemented are described below.

DAYTON, OHIO

Dayton, Ohio, is heavily dependent upon ground water to meet municipal and industrial water-supply needs. Nearly one-fourth of all ground water used in Ohio is withdrawn from wells completed in a sole-source sand and gravel aquifer that underlies the Dayton metropolitan area. Much of the water is pumped from a 30- to 75-foot thick shallow aquifer that underlies the Mad River Valley. To ensure that ground-water levels are maintained high enough to allow for large drawdowns by high-capacity wells, an artificial recharge system has been in place since the 1930's. The source of recharge is streamflow diverted from the Mad River into a series of interconnected infiltration ditches and lagoons that occupy about 20 acres on Rohrers Island. To meet increasing demand, a new municipal well field was developed in the 1960's in a section of the aquifer north of Dayton. Here, water is pumped from the Great Miami River into a series of ponds and lagoons, some of which also serve as water hazards on a city-owned golf course. Recharge lagoons at both well fields are periodically drained, and accumulated muck and silt are excavated to maintain a high rate of infiltration into the underlying aquifer.

High-capacity turbine pump installed on a municipal well at Rohrers Island. Recharge lagoon in background. (Photograph by Brent Means, U.S. Geological Survey.)

ORLANDO, FLORIDA

Large volumes of reclaimed water, which has undergone advanced secondary treatment, are reused through land-based applications in a 40-square-mile area near Orlando, Florida. These applications include citrus crop irrigation and artificial recharge to the surficial aquifer through rapid infiltration basins.

Rapid infiltration basins. (Photograph courtesy of Water Conserv II facility, Orlando, Florida.)

ORANGE COUNTY, CALIFORNIA

Orange County, near Los Angeles, California, receives an average of only 13 to 15 inches of rainfall annually, yet sustains a population of approximately 2.5 million people. A ground-water basin that underlies the northwestern half of the county supplies about 75 percent of the total water demand. As the area developed from a thriving agricultural center into a highly urbanized area, increased demands for ground water resulted in a gradual lowering of the water table below sea level and encroachment of saltwater from the Pacific Ocean. To prevent further saltwater intrusion and to replenish the ground-water supply, the Orange County Water District operates a hydraulic barrier system composed of a series of 23 multipoint wells that inject freshwater into the aquifer, blocking further passage of seawater. The source of injection water is a blended combination of deep well water and recycled secondary effluent. The recycled product meets drinking-water standards through advanced treatment processes of reverse osmosis and activated carbon adsorption.

Wildwood beach in the summer. (Photograph courtesy of Cape May County Division of Tourism.)

Water Factory 21 treatment facility. (Photograph courtesy of Orange County Water District.)

WILDWOOD, NEW JERSEY

Wildwood, New Jersey, is a resort town on a barrier island along the Atlantic Coast. As a resort community, it has a large influx of tourists in the summertime. The population can increase from about 5,000 during the winter to 30,000 at the height of the summer tourist season. The Wildwood Water Utility withdraws water from wells located about 5 miles inland from the barrier island. To supply water from these wells to meet the island's needs during the summer would require a large pumping facility and transmission lines that would be little used the rest of the year. To avoid these excessive costs, the utility injects ground water into a shallow aquifer on the island during periods of low demand and withdraws the water in the summer by using dual injection and recovery wells. This system, operated since 1967, represents perhaps the oldest operational aquifer storage recovery (ASR) project in the United States. In ASR, water is injected underground, commonly into nonpotable or saline aquifers, where it forms a lens of good quality water for later recovery from the same well(s). Operation of a typical ASR installation is designed to smooth out annual variability in water demand by recharging aquifers during periods of low demand and recovering the water during periods of high demand. Advantages of ASR over other artificial recharge schemes are that it uses very little land (especially compared to surface spreading) and reduces the cost and maintenance of separate injection and recovery wells.

LONG ISLAND, NEW YORK

Ground water is the sole source of freshwater for the more than 3 million people who live on Long Island outside the metropolitan New York City boundary. (The Long Island ground-water system was discussed earlier in the sections on "Ground-Water Development, Sustainability, and Water Budgets" and "Effects of Ground-Water Development on Ground-Water Storage.") To help replenish the aquifer, as well as reduce urban flooding and control saltwater intrusion, more than 3,000 recharge basins dispose of storm runoff at an average rate of about 150 million gallons per day. Initially, many of these basins were abandoned gravel pits, but since 1936 urban developers are required to provide recharge basins with new developments. Practically all basins are unlined excavations in the upper glacial deposits and have areas from less than 0.1 to more than 30 acres.

Aerial photograph of development on Long Island showing recharge basin. (Photograph courtesy of Nassau County Department of Public Works.)

Concluding Remarks

In conclusion, we would like to emphasize the following interrelated facts and concepts:

- The most important and most extensively discussed concept in this report is that volumes of water pumped from a ground-water system must come from somewhere and must cause a change in the ground-water system. Possible sources of water for pumpage are (1) more water entering the ground-water system (increased recharge), (2) less water leaving the system (decreased discharge), and (3) removal of water that was stored in the system.

- One of the critical linkages in both unstressed and stressed ground-water systems is between ground water and surface water. Pumping water from aquifers that are hydraulically connected with surface-water bodies can have a significant effect on those bodies by reducing ground-water discharges to surface water and possibly causing outflow from those bodies into the ground-water system. Thus, an evaluation of ground-water management strategies needs to involve consideration of surface-water resources, including closely related biological resources.

- A key feature of some aquifers and ground-water systems is the large volume of ground water in storage, which allows the possibility of using aquifers for temporary storage, that is, managing inflow and outflow of ground water in storage in a manner similar to surface-water reservoirs.

- From the standpoint of water use and water management, all ground water is not equal—the suitability of water, as measured by its quality, is a key consideration in developing water-management strategies. Furthermore, determining water suitability (or unsuitability) requires detailed information on the three-dimensional distribution and concentrations of potential contaminants, both naturally occurring contaminants and those resulting from human activities.

- Continuing large withdrawals of water from an aquifer often result in undesirable consequences. The most common of these consequences have been discussed throughout this report. From a management standpoint, water managers, stakeholders, and the public must decide the specific conditions under which the undesirable consequences can no longer be tolerated.

- The effects of ground-water development may require many years to become evident. Thus, there is an unfortunate tendency to forego the data collection and analysis that is needed to support informed decision making until well after problems materialize.

- Evaluation of possible ground-water management approaches (a) depends on the continuing collection, archiving, and analysis of a broad range of different types of information, and (b) can be assisted by well-designed computer simulation models.

ACKNOWLEDGMENTS

Technical review of this Circular was provided by John Vecchioli, J.W. LaBaugh, W.W. Lapham, S.A. Leake, and T.C. Winter. G.J. Beserra, M.J. Focazio, Cindy Gehman, P.D. Hays, R.E. Krause, P.J. Lacombe, V.L. McGuire, Jack Monti, D.S. Morgan, L.C. Murray, A.S. Navoy, D.L. Nelms, G.B. Ozuna, G.L. Rowe, M.P. Scorca, A.G. Spinello, and D.K. Yobbi provided information for some of the examples. J.V. Flager, M.A. Kidd, and Chet Zenone provided editorial and technical reviews. The final manuscript was prepared by M.J. VanAlstine, J.K. Monson, J.M. Evans, R.J. Olmstead, E.J. Swibas, and C.L. Anderson.

REFERENCES

Alley, W.M., and Emery, P.A., 1986, Groundwater model of the Blue River Basin, Nebraska—Twenty years later: Journal of Hydrology, v. 85, p. 225–249.

Alley, W.M., and Schefter, J.E., 1987, External effects of irrigator's pumping decisions, High Plains aquifer: Water Resources Research, v. 23, no. 7, p. 1123–1130.

American Society of Civil Engineers, 1969, Saltwater intrusion in the United States: Journal of the Hydraulics Division Proceedings of the ASCE, v. 95, no. HY5, p. 1651–1669.

Avery, C.F., 1995, Reversal of declining ground-water levels in the Chicago area: U.S. Geological Survey Fact Sheet 222–95, 2 p.

Bacchus, S.T., 1998, Determining sustainable yield for karst aquifers of the southeastern coastal plain— A need for new approaches, *in* Borchers, J.W., ed., Land subsidence case studies and current research, Proceedings of the Dr. Joseph F. Poland Symposium on Land Subsidence: Association of Engineering Geologists, Special Publication no. 8, p. 503–519.

Beattie, B.R., 1981, Irrigated agriculture and the Great Plains—Problems and management alternatives: Western Journal of Agricultural Economics, v. 6, no. 2, p. 289–299.

Bredehoeft, J.D., Papadopulos, S.S., and Cooper, H.H. Jr., 1982, Groundwater—The water-budget myth, *in* Scientific basis of water-resource management: National Academy Press, p. 51–57.

Carpenter, M.C., in press, South-central Arizona, *in* Galloway, D., Jones, D., and Ingebritsen, S., eds., Land subsidence in the United States: U.S. Geological Survey Circular 1182.

Carter, Virginia, 1996, Wetland hydrology, water quality, and associated functions, *in* National water summary—Wetland resources: U.S. Geological Survey Water-Supply Paper 2425, 431 p.

Cederstrom, D.J., 1945, Geology and ground-water resources of the Coastal Plain in southeastern Virginia: Virginia Geological Survey Bulletin 63, 384 p.

Cohen, P., Franke, O.L., and Foxworthy, B.L., 1968, An atlas of Long Island's water resources: New York Water Resources Commission Bulletin 62, 117 p.

Downing, R.A. (compiler), 1998, Groundwater our hidden asset: Earthwise Series, British Geological Survey, Keyworth, Nottingham, UK, 59 p.

Emery, P.A., 1965, Effect of ground-water pumping on streamflow and ground-water levels, Blue River Basin, Nebraska: U.S. Geological Survey Open-File Report, 11 p.

Franke, O.L., and McClymonds, N.E., 1972, Summary of the hydrologic situation on Long Island, New York, as a guide to water-management alternatives: U.S. Geological Survey Professional Paper 627–F, 59 p.

Galloway, D., Jones, D., and Ingebritsen, S., eds., in press, Land subsidence in the United States: U.S. Geological Survey Circular 1182.

Galloway, D., and Riley, F.S., in press, San Joaquin Valley, California, *in* Galloway, D., Jones, D., and Ingebritsen, S., eds., Land subsidence in the United States: U.S. Geological Survey Circular 1182.

Gelt, J., Henderson, J, Seasholes, K., Tellman, B., Woodard, G., and others, 1999, Water in the Tucson area: Seeking sustainability: Water Resources Research Center, University of Arizona, Issue Paper #20, 155 p.

Gutentag, E.D., Heimes, F.J., Krothe, N.C., Luckey, R.R., and Weeks, J.B., 1984, Geohydrology of the High Plains aquifer in parts of Colorado, Kansas, Nebraska, New Mexico, Oklahoma, South Dakota, Texas, and Wyoming: U.S. Geological Survey Professional Paper 1400–B, 63 p.

Heath, R.C., 1983, Basic ground-water hydrology: U.S. Geological Survey Water-Supply Paper 2220, 84 p.

Hubbell, J.M., Bishop, C.W., Johnson, G.S., and Lucas, J.G., 1997, Numerical ground-water flow modeling of the Snake River Plain aquifer using the super-position technique: Ground Water, v. 35, no. 1, p. 59–66.

Hunt, R.J., Walker, J.F., and Krabbenhoft, D.P., 1999, Characterizing hydrology and the importance of ground-water discharge in natural and constructed wetlands: Wetlands, v. 19, no. 2, p. 458–472.

Johnson, M.S., and Pederson, D.T., 1983, Groundwater levels in Nebraska, 1982: Lincoln, University of Nebraska, Conservation and Survey Division, Nebraska Water Survey Paper 56, 65 p.

Johnston, R.H., 1989, The hydrologic responses to development in regional sedimentary aquifers: Ground Water, v. 27, no. 3, p. 316–322.

Konikow, L.F., and Bredehoeft, J.D., 1992, Ground-water models cannot be validated: Advances in Water Resources, v. 15, p. 75–83.

Konikow, L.F., and Reilly, T.E., 1999, Groundwater modeling, *in* Delleur, J.W., ed., The handbook of groundwater engineering: Boca Raton, Fla., CRC Press, p. 20-1—20-40.

Lohman, S.W., 1972, Ground-water hydraulics: U.S. Geological Survey Professional Paper 708, 70 p.

Luckey, R.R., Gutentag, E.D., Heimes, F.J., and Weeks, J.B., 1986, Digital simulation of the ground-water flow in the High Plains aquifer in parts of Colorado, Kansas, Nebraska, New Mexico, Oklahoma, South Dakota, Texas, and Wyoming: U.S. Geological Survey Professional Paper 1400-D, 57 p.

McGrail, L., Berk, K., Brandes, D., Munch, D., Neubauer, C., Osburn, W., Rao, D., Thomson, J., and Toth, D., 1998, St. Johns River Water Management District, *in* Fernald, E.A., and Purdum, E.D., eds., Water resources atlas of Florida: Tallahassee, Florida State University, Institute of Science and Public Affairs, p. 214–237.

McGuire, V.L., and Sharpe, J.B., 1997, Water-level changes in the High Plains aquifer—Predevelopment to 1995: U.S. Geological Survey Water-Resources Investigations Report 97–4081, 2 pl.

Morgan, D.S., and Jones, J.L., 1999, Numerical model analysis of the effects of ground-water withdrawals on discharge to streams and springs in small basins typical of the Puget Sound Lowland, Washington: U.S. Geological Survey Water-Supply Paper 2492, 73 p.

Morris, E.E., and Bush, W.V., 1986, Extent and source of saltwater intrusion into the alluvial aquifer near Brinkley, Arkansas, 1984: U.S. Geological Survey Water-Resources Investigations Report 85–4322, 123 p.

Nace, R.L., 1960, Water management, agriculture, and ground-water supplies: U.S. Geological Survey Circular 415, 12 p.

Plummer, L.N., Busenberg, E., McConnell, J.B., Drenkard, S., Schlosser, P., and Michel, R.L., 1998, Flow of river water into a karstic limestone aquifer. 1. Tracing the young fraction in ground-water mixtures in the Upper Floridan aquifer near Valdosta, Georgia: Applied Geochemistry, v. 13, no. 8, p. 995–1015.

Reilly, T.E., and Pollock, D.W., 1993, Factors affecting areas contributing recharge to wells in shallow aquifers: U.S. Geological Survey Water-Supply Paper 2412, 21 p.

Schaefer, F.L., and Walker, R.L., 1981, Saltwater intrusion into the Old Bridge aquifer in the Keyport-Union Beach area of Monmouth County, New Jersey: U.S. Geological Survey Water-Supply Paper 2184, 21 p.

Solley, W.B., 1995, United States Geological Survey National Water-Use Information Program: U.S. Geological Survey Fact Sheet FS–057–95, 4 p.

Solley, W.B., Pierce, R.R., and Perlman, H.A., 1998, Estimated use of water in the United States in 1995: U.S. Geological Survey Circular 1200, 71 p.

Sophocleous, M., ed., 1998, Perspectives on sustainable development of water resources in Kansas: Kansas Geological Survey Bulletin 239, 239 p.

Spinello, A.G., and Simmons, D.L., 1992, Base flow of 10 south-shore streams, Long Island, New York, 1976–85, and the effects of urbanization on base flow and flow duration: U.S. Geological Survey Water-Resources Investigations Report 90–4205, 34 p.

Sun, R.J., ed., 1986, Regional Aquifer-System Analysis Program of the U.S. Geological Survey—Summary of projects, 1978–84: U.S. Geological Survey Circular 1002, 264 p.

Swanson, A.A., 1998, Land subsidence in the San Joaquin Valley, updated to 1995, *in* Borchers, J.W., ed., Land subsidence case studies and current research: Proceedings of the Dr. Joseph F. Poland Symposium on Land Subsidence, Sacramento, Calif., October 4–5, 1995, Association of Engineering Geologists, Special Publication no. 8, p. 75–79.

Theis, C.V., 1940, The source of water derived from wells: Civil Engineering, v. 10, no. 5, p. 277–280.

U.S. Geological Survey, 1984, National water summary 1983—Hydrologic events and issues: U.S. Geological Survey Water-Supply Paper 2250, 243 p.

U.S. Geological Survey, 1998, Strategic directions for the U.S. Geological Survey Ground-Water Resources Program: A report to Congress, November 30, 1998, 14 p.

U.S. Water Resources Council, 1980, Essentials of ground-water hydrology pertinent to water-resources planning: U.S. Water Resources Council Hydrology Committee Bulletin 16 (revised), 38 p.

Visocky, A.P., 1997, Water-level trends and pumpage in the deep bedrock aquifers in the Chicago region, 1991–1995: Illinois State Water Survey, Champaign, Circular 182.

Walton, W.C., 1964, Future water-level declines in deep sandstone wells in Chicago region: Ground Water, v. 2, no. 1, p. 13–20.

Winter, T.C., Harvey, J.W., Franke, O.L., and Alley, W.M., 1998, Ground water and surface water— A single resource: U.S. Geological Survey Circular 1139, 79 p.

☆ U.S. GOVERNMENT PRINTING OFFICE: 1999 — 773-052 / 24013 Region No. 8